MEMOS
FROM THE
CHAIRMAN

MEMOS
FROM THE
CHAIRMAN

BY ALAN C. GREENBERG

WITH A FOREWORD BY
WARREN BUFFETT

Workman Publishing, New York

Library of Congress Cataloging-in-Publication Data
Greenberg, Alan C.
Memos from the chairman/by Alan C. Greenberg; with a foreword by Warren Buffett.
p. cm.
ISBN-13: 978-0-7611-0346-2; ISBN-10: 0-7611-0346-5
1. Business writing. 2. Memorandums—Humor. I. Title.
HF5718.3G74   1996
658.4'53'0207—dc20   96-2481   CIP

The author's proceeds from the sale of this book will benefit
the Alan C. Greenberg Scholarship Fund. Beneficiaries are Bear Stearns
employees or their relatives.

Workman Publishing
708 Broadway
New York, New York 10003-9555

Manufactured in the United States of America
First printing March 1996
10

Ace Greenberg does almost everything better than I do—
bridge, magic tricks, dog training, arbitrage—all the important things
in life. He so excels at these that you might think it would give deep
inferiority complexes to his colleagues at Bear Stearns. But if you
think that, you don't know much about his colleagues.

In this book we finally learn where all this wit and wisdom—and
there's plenty of both—come from: Haimchinkel Malintz Anaynikal.
(I used to have trouble pronouncing his last name until I learned that the
trick is to rhyme it with Ahaynikal.) Haimchinkel sees all, knows all, and
tells all—but only through Ace, his Designated Oracle here on earth.

Haimchinkel is my kind of guy—cheap, smart, opinionated.
I just wish I'd met him earlier in life, when, in the foolishness of youth,
I used to discard paper clips. But it's never too late, and I now slavishly
follow and preach his principles.

Many years ago, *Where Are the Customers' Yachts?*, through a
humorous look at Wall Street, dispensed some of the best investment
advice ever written. In this book, Ace has applied the same treatment to
managerial advice with equal success.

WARREN BUFFETT
January 1996

CONTENTS

1978–1988

From the time of its founding in 1923, to 1978, Bear Stearns changed from a small commission house to an important factor in the securities industry and expanded into many areas, including those that risked capital. The driving force behind that growth and expansion was Cy Lewis, who assumed leadership of the firm in 1936. On April 26, 1978 he suffered a massive stroke and died two days later; so we started our fiscal year on May 1, 1978 without the man who was credited with having made Bear Stearns what it then was. It was the prevalent thought on Wall Street that, without Cy Lewis, Bear Stearns would fade away like nomads in the night. Those skeptics overlooked one of Cy's main attributes. He encouraged and promoted young people as fast as they warranted it. He left a group that could and *did* carry on.

As the new chief executive officer, I knew I needed help

to implement policies that had been running through my mind for some time. It was at this point that I met Haimchinkel Malintz Anaynikal, the dean of business philosophers, who immediately became my mentor and adviser. Through memos to my associates, I communicated his wisdom and ideas about how best to strengthen our bottom line.

These memos cover the ten years from May 1978 to May 1988. They may give you some idea of our growth and the fun we had participating in the further building of Bear Stearns. Although they seem to have been written in jest, I can assure you that the points I was trying to make in these communications were things I believed in very strongly and still do. There are many ways to run and build a firm. I used those memos to express my philosophies, and, in our case, I think they worked.

.

Memo

To　　All General & Limited Partners　　Date　　October 5, 1978

From　　Alan C. Greenberg　　CC

Subject

    Bear Stearns is moving forward at an accelerated rate and everybody is contributing. It is absolutely essential for us to be able to talk to our partners at all times. All of us are entitled to eat lunch, play golf and go on vacation. But, you must leave word with your secretary or associates where you can be reached at all times. Decisions have to be made and your input can be important!

    I conducted a study of the 200 firms that have disappeared from Wall Street over the last few years, and I discovered that 62.349% went out of business because the important people did not leave word where they went when they left their desk if even for 10 minutes.

    That idiocy will not occur here.

Memo

To   All General & Limited Partners   Date   March 13, 1979

From   Alan C. Greenberg   CC

Subject

The Executive Committee last night approved a group of people who who will be asked to become Limited Partners of Bear, Stearns & Co., subject to the approval of the other General Partners. You will be receiving this list shortly.

Carl Holstrom has just informed me that we have signed a $12 million long-term loan agreement with a major insurance company. This will replace our loan with the First National Bank of Chicago. The implications and the actual dollar savings of this agreement are of tremendous importance to Bear, Stearns & Co.

I also just received the P and L results for February and, in my opinion, they were great. These three items will be covered in detail at the Partners' Meeting on March 19th.

The developments at Bear Stearns certainly seem to be positive and as a result we will, of course, intensify our surveillance of all positions and expenses. You know how I feel about the dangers of overconfidence.

It certainly looks like we have a dynamic future in store as long as we remember the words of the famous philosopher, Haimchinkel Malintz Anaynikal: "thou will do well in commerce as long as thou does not believe thine own odor is perfume."

Memo

BEAR STEARNS

To · All General & Limited Partners and Other Potential Perfume Lovers

Date · March 23, 1979

From · Eclectic Thoughts from the Complete Works of Haimchinkel Malintz Anaynikal

CC

Subject

Witter Has Deficit of $886,000

The Dean Witter Reynolds Organization Inc., which operates a worldwide securities firm, reported yesterday a loss of $886,000 for the second fiscal quarter ended Feb. 28 and a profit of $2.5 million, or 28 cents a share, for the six months.

In the year-earlier quarter, net income was $713,000, or 9 cents a share, and in the six-month period, net was $3 million, or 49 cents a share, on fewer shares outstanding. The company noted, however, that the figures for the previous year's periods included results for the combined companies for only two months.

The company was formed Jan. 3, 1978, through the consolidation of the Dean Witter Organization and Reynolds Securities International, in one of the largest mergers in brokerage history.

Revenues in the quarter increased to $114 million from $81.1 million, while for the six months they jumped to $244.2 million from $141.4 million, again

with combined results for only two months.

Results Termed Unsatisfactory

William M. Witter, chairman, said: "We are not satisfied with the performance of Dean Witter Reynolds Inc., our principal subsidiary, during the second quarter when its revenues declined by about $17 million from the previous first quarter. However, that unit's performance must be measured against a background where the markets tended to be treacherous and activity deceptively low."

The firm continues to make substantial investments in advertising, operational improvements and in physical facilities, Mr. Witter declared.

Directors of the organization authorized the repurchase of up to 400,000 shares of outstanding common stock. These shares could be used for stock options and general corporate purposes, the company stated.

(from The Wall Street Journal)

Memo

To	All General & Limited Partners	Date	June 15, 1979
From	Alan C. Greenberg	CC	
Subject			

During the last few days, the newspapers have devoted a lot of space to the profits generated by the New York Stock Exchange Member Firms during the period of January, February and March of 1979. I thought you might like to know how we did using the same yardstick.

Comparison of Focus
1st Quarter Calendar 1979
($000)

	Bear Stearns	Industry	Bear Stearns as % of Industry
Revenues	$51,595	$2,430,700	2.1%
Expenses	40,280	2,197,000	1.8%
Income Before Taxes	11,315	233,700	4.8%

I would also like to add that the last three weeks have been a thing of beauty. Every department is really boiling and some of the new people that we have taken on are starting to make real contributions.

Because of this good news, I think it is time for us once again to spend some time reading the works of, and reflecting on the thoughts of, Haimchinkel Malintz Anaynikal.

Memo

BEAR STEARNS

To   All General & Limited Partners   Date   January 30, 1980

From   Alan C. Greenberg   CC

Subject

Several of my partners have spoken to me during this last week about the remarkable way things seem to be falling in place for us. Some of the things that have happened to us have been due to our own efforts, but equally, some of our good fortune of late has been due to luck.

I have been around long enough to know that the shoe usually falls on your head when you least expect it. All of these factors have made me reflect on the words of Haimchinkel Malintz Anaynikal. I have taken the liberty of quoting in full from the last two paragraphs of my memo dated March 13, 1979.

> "The developments at Bear Stearns certainly seem to be positive and as a result, we will, of course, intensify our surveillance of all positions and expenses. You know how I feel about the dangers of overconfidence.
>
> It certainly looks like we have a dynamic future in store as long as we remember the words of the famous philosopher, Haimchinkel Malintz Anaynikal, 'thou will do well in commerce as long as thou does not believe thine own odor is perfume.'"

Memo

BEAR STEARNS

To   All General & Limited Partners   Date   May 28, 1980

From   Alan C. Greenberg   CC

Subject

The month of May was the first month of our new fiscal year and for bookkeeping purposes it ended on May 22nd. Preliminary indications are that it appears to be the best month in the history of Bear Stearns.

Before we get carried away, there is one thing that I do want to emphasize. We are working with more capital than ever before, so if every month is not a record-breaker, we are probably getting lazy. We have plenty of room for improvement and there are still a number of leaks in the dike. In fact, the only area that I think is running at 100% efficiency is the error account.

I implore our partners who supervise salesmen to increase their surveillance of all personnel. I want all partners in the trading area to pay particular attention that our positions do not increase dramatically in size and that we continue to assiduously follow the rules of Haimchinkel Malintz Anaynikal in the area of loss-taking, freshness of positions and body perfume.*

I have, of course, asked Carl Holstrom to once again tighten all surveillance of expense accounts for partners and our associates. You should also be hearing shortly from Marvin Davidson about our ballooning departmental expenses.

It is up to all of us to fight our unrelenting enemies—complacency, over-confidence and conceit.

* For those of you who might have forgotten Haimchinkel Malintz Anaynikal's comments on this subject, ask Peggy Moynihan for my memo dated 3/13/79.

Memo

To   All General & Limited Partners   Date   October 17, 1980

From   Alan C. Greenberg   CC

Subject

October 16th was the fifth biggest day in the history of the New York Stock Exchange. It was the biggest day in Bear Stearns' history by about 20%. I am referring to both number of tickets and overall commission revenues.

Our increase in market share is certainly something to be proud of, but cooperation with the Operations personnel has become more critical than ever. Please make it a point that the people who work with you do everything to help operational personnel whenever they come in contact with them.

I would also like to point out that the philosophy and works of Haimchinkel Malintz Anaynikal are once again "must" reading. If you misplaced your copy, please call Peggy Moynihan on extension 5369.

Memo

BEAR
STEARNS

To   All General & Limited Partners   Date   May 5, 1981

From   Alan C. Greenberg   CC

Subject

There has been a lot of publicity lately about firms hiring students with MBA degrees. I think it is important that we continue a policy that has helped us prosper while growing from 700 people eight years ago to over 2,600 today.

Our first desire is to promote from within. If somebody with an MBA degree applies for a job, we will certainly not hold it against them, but we are really looking for people with PSD* degrees. They built this firm and there are plenty around because our competition seems to be restricting themselves to MBA's.

If we are smart, we will end up with the future Cy Lewises, Gus Levys and Bunny Laskers. These men made their mark with a high school degree and a PSD.

* PSD stands for poor, smart and a deep desire to become rich.

Memo

BEAR STEARNS

To   General Partners   Date   August 20, 1982

From   Alan C. Greenberg   CC

Subject

Every partner is entitled to a vacation, and we have never been particularly fussy about how long the vacation is nor do we keep score on how much time is taken over the course of the year. I do feel that if a partner is not on vacation, he should treat Friday like any other day and show up for a full day's work.

Haimchinkel Malintz Anaynikal never took off a Friday in his entire life.

Memo

To	All General & Limited Partners	Date	October 5, 1982
From	Alan C. Greenberg	CC	

Subject

September looks like it was the best month in the history of Bear Stearns. The past four weeks appear to be particularly gratifying because I think every area contributed and it demonstrated what so many of us have been saying about our potential if conditions changed for the better.

After a month like the one we just experienced, I think we should be on our guard against the negatives that go along with great success. I am speaking of complacency, sloppiness, relaxing on expenses, cockiness and just getting careless in general.

This is the time to be on our guard. If the market does go our way, I want to make every dollar and leave nothing on the table. The market may turn sour again, so do not forget for a moment what the great coach Haimchinkel Malintz Anaynikal said many years ago, "when the going gets tough, the tough start selling."

Our firm has dynamic money-making potential and will continue to grow and prosper beyond our wildest dreams if we devote all of our working hours to Bear, Stearns & Co. This has led the Executive Committee to decide that no General Partners or General Partners' spouses can make any outside investments (other than publicly traded stocks and bonds or a residence) without the approval of the Executive Committee. The Executive Committee does not want our partners worrying or thinking about any business other than Bear Stearns. Owning an equity interest in our firm is the best investment any of us will ever see; so let us give B.S. 100% of our effort.

Memo

To   All General & Limited Partners   Date   January 10, 1983

From   Alan C. Greenberg   CC

Subject Error Account

We must have a great business, because I think we broke even last week after paying for a horrendous series of errors. I am well aware that humans will always make errors. My irritation comes from the fact that these errors are not caught immediately. In many cases, this is because the producer is too lazy to look at his run the following day; too lazy to look at the registered representative copies of the confirms and too lazy to check the monthly statements.

The firm has always been very understanding when errors are made. We will not be understanding if the error is not caught because of subsequent stupidity and laziness.

Please see that the people who work with and for you understand the rules because I do not want any crying when an associate blows a year's salary.

You are aware that I have said for years that complacency is our greatest enemy. Is this the first symptom of our decadence? If it is, I know how to cure this form of sloppiness.

Memo

To	All General & Limited Partners	Date	May 2, 1983
From	Alan C. Greenberg	CC	

Subject

Haimchinkel Malintz Anaynikal just called and reminded me of something that I should have thought of without any help.

The year was over last Friday and it was a good one, but last year is gone. The score right now is nothing to nothing. Nobody cares (especially our competition) what we did last year.

Let us go to the whip and make the month of May an indication of what we are going to do for the coming twelve months.

Memo

BEAR STEARNS

To   All Personnel   Date   June 22, 1983

From   Alan C. Greenberg   CC

Subject Incoming Mail, Packages, Carrier Pigeons, and other methods of transport pertaining to items delivered to the premises of Bear Stearns.

New York Stock Exchange Rules require that we open and examine all incoming mail before it is distributed to the addressee. "Incoming mail" includes items and packages delivered to the firm by hand or picked up by our messenger service. All packages delivered to the firm are to be opened and the contents inspected. Bear Stearns has followed this directive in the past and we will follow it much more assiduously in the future.

We are tripling our inspection capability. The reason for this is that a package we recently opened was found to contain "contraband." The item was confiscated and destroyed. The next time we find anyone sending or receiving any such matter at Bear Stearns, we will notify the proper authorities. Regardless of the action taken by the police, Bear Stearns will show no mercy. An example will be made of the next and future offenders.

If anyone does not understand this memo, please come and see me and I will explain it personally!

Memo

To	All General Partners	Date	June 24, 1983
From	Alan C. Greenberg	CC	

Subject

On October 5, 1978, the attached memo was distributed. We have been very successful since that memo was issued, and I think that 93.4% of our success has been due to the instant availability of our partners and associates.

During the past month, we have been very busy and some of us have been straying away from the fundamentals, such as leaving word at all times where they may be found. We must not deviate from the basics.

I have contacted Marlin Perkins of the St. Louis Zoo and the next person that I have trouble finding will be fitted out with a radio collar. Please impress our policy on the people who work with and under you. The collars are bulky and not very attractive.

Memo

To   All General & Limited Partners   Date   September 9, 1983

From   Alan C. Greenberg   CC

Subject

Haimchinkel Malintz Anaynikal just called and told me he was very impressed with the results for the month of August. I have not seen them yet, but if they are as good as Haimchinkel Malintz Anaynikal thinks they are, then August was probably the best month we have ever had in relative terms.

The bond market and the stock market did nothing, but the Bear Stearns machine did its thing. His call, however, reminded me of the warning he gave us some years ago, "thou will do well in commerce as long as thou does not believe thine own odor is perfume." I assured him that despite our success, we are still trying to be as careful and as punctilious as always.

DO NOT MAKE A LIAR OUT OF ME.

Memo

BEAR STEARNS

To	All General & Limited Partners	Date	January 25, 1984
From	Alan C. Greenberg	CC	

Subject

You have probably seen the published results of our competitors for the past three months. You are also probably up to date on how we have done for the past three months and the first eight months of this fiscal year.

Observing these figures makes me more determined than ever to follow the simple rules laid down by the Dean of Business Philosophers, Haimchinkel Malintz Anaynikal:

1- Stick to thine own business.

2- Watch thy shop.

3- Limit thy losses.

4- Watch thy expenses like a hawk.

5- Stay humble, humble, humble.

6- When dealing with a new account, know thy customer and know thy customer's money is up.

At the partners meeting two weeks ago, it was pointed out to me by Haimchinkel Malintz Anaynikal that the hors d'oeuvres had been upgraded considerably from peanuts. You will be happy to know that we are now back to peanuts. This may seem like a small saving, but it's the thought that counts.

Memo

To   All General & Limited Partners   Date   April 10, 1984

From   Sir Alan C. Greenberg   CC

Subject

The figures for the month of March were just given to me. We have had better months in absolute terms, but on a relative basis I think last month's performance was the best I have ever seen. I also think that our record for the first three months of 1984 is something to be proud of because the markets were down, difficult and dangerous at best.

Haimchinkel Malintz Anaynikal recently brought to my attention certain intercompany feuds that have led to the downfall of firms smarter, richer and larger than ours. Watching for these signs of dissension will be a high priority of mine.

Whenever you have a partnership of over 80 people, there is bound to be a person or two who is not your exact cup of yogurt. For years, the partners of this firm have gotten along remarkably well and the cooperation at this time is great. One of the things I am going to be extremely sensitive about in the future—and come down very hard on when I see or hear of it—is acrimony among partners. Honest men may differ, but when the difference becomes animosity, you can have problems. I am not going to let personal conflicts have any effect on the net income of our golden goose.

The year is not over yet and we have 20 days left to make this one to be proud of. Hope to see all of you in person at the Annual Meeting.

Memo

To	ALL REGISTERED REPRESENTATIVES	Date	JULY 23, 1984
From	ALAN C. GREENBERG	CC	

Subject

These are tough times. The market has been extremely difficult since last July. It is certainly no fun to walk in on a Monday morning and get hit with a twelve-point decline.

I hope all of you know how important I think you are to Bear Stearns and how I empathize with what you are going through.

It is important to me that every department that interreacts with the Registered Representatives give 100% support now more than ever to the efforts and desires of the Registered Representatives.

You will be doing me a favor if you call me immediately anytime you think you are getting less than Triple A treatment.

The support areas are under extreme pressure, but that will never be an excuse for not treating our sales force in the manner they deserve.

Memo

To   All General & Limited Partners   Date   July 25, 1984

From   Alan C. Greenberg   CC

Subject

The newspapers are full of the quarterly financial results of the publicly owned investment banking firms. For the three months ended June 30th, Bear, Stearns & Co. had a loss of $3,473,000, after interest on partners' capital.

That figure will not help you buy much from Tiffany, but it does mean that we are keeping things under reasonable control. Keep in mind that the figures of our corporate competitors are usually after tax credits. For example, the loss of $33 million by Merrill, Lynch, reported this morning, was really $90 million before tax credits.

We are not panicking; we are not laying off people, but we are making a real effort to cut expenses. The other side of the coin is we have hired a large number of number one draft picks in the last few months. This is the time to hire good people. We have followed this policy in the past, and I am convinced that we will be proven correct once again.

I did not want to write this memo, but Haimchinkel Malintz Anaynikal insisted that I communicate with the troops, even when the news is less than perfect. Haimchinkel Malintz Anaynikal also mentioned that now is the time _not_ to hide from clients. It takes real courage to make calls when you know the reception might be hostile. But there are times when we must face the music. It will pay off when the market turns, and I promise you the market will turn. I hope sooner rather than later.

Memo

BEAR STEARNS

To	All General & Limited Partners	Date	June 19, 1985

From   Alan C. Greenberg   CC

Subject

The month of May is history, but it looks like we did get ten runs in the first inning. I frankly cannot remember any time in the past where we ever broke even in the month of May, much less made money.

Haimchinkel Malintz dropped down, saw the figures and made some suggestions. We should not lose sight of fundamentals, such as cutting expenses and being ever alert to the fact that if we are not careful, there are some people who would like to steal the whole place out from under us.

He pointed out to me that the tendency is to cut expenses when things are tough and how stupid that line of reasoning is. When things are good, you should be even more careful of expenses because it is ridiculous to leave anything on the table when you hold a royal flush. We must continue to be alert, aggressive and never complacent. And last, but maybe most important, the partners of this firm must continue to work together and learn to overlook petty differences. We are all expendable and I hope that your Executive Committee does not have to prove that to any of us.

Memo

BEAR STEARNS

To   GENERAL & LIMITED PARTNERS   Date   August 9, 1985

From   Alan C. Greenberg   CC

Subject **EXPENSES**

I was just shown the results for our first quarter. They were excellent. When mortals go through a prosperous period, it seems to be human nature for expenses to balloon. We are going to be the exception. I have just informed the purchasing department that they should no longer purchase paper clips. All of us receive documents every day with paper clips on them. If we save these paper clips, not only will we have enough for our own use, but we will also, in a short time, be awash in the little critters. Periodically, we will collect excess paper clips and sell them (since the cost to us is zero, the Arbitrage Department tells me the return on capital will be above average). This action may seem a little petty, but anything we can do to make our people conscious of expenses is worthwhile.

In addition to the paper clip caper, we also are going to cut down on ordering the blue envelopes used for interoffice mail. These envelopes can be used over and over again. All of us are going to help our bottom line grow.

Bear Stearns is probably going to sell stock to the public, and there is one guarantee that I would like to give the potential buyers of our stock—they are going to get the fairest shake from us that management can give any public shareholder. This place is going to be run tight, and the reasons are not all altruistic. We are not going public for the perks. We are going public for a number of reasons, and one is that we want the stock to appreciate.

You have probably guessed by now that these thoughts are not original. They came from one of Haimchinkel Malintz Anaynikal's earlier works. His thoughts have not exactly steered us wrong so far. Let's stick with his theories till he lets us down.

Memo

To	GENERAL & LIMITED PARTNERS	Date August 15, 1985
From	Alan C. Greenberg	CC

Subject **GETTING RICHER**

Thank you, thank you, thank you! The response to the memo on paper clips and envelopes has been overwhelming. It seems that we already have an excess of paper clips. This excess will be picked up shortly by a designated paper-clipper-picker-upper person and, of course, will be sold through competitive bidding.

Because of your cooperation, I would like to extend our cost-cutting efforts to a larger matter. Bear Stearns will no longer purchase rubber bands. If we can save paper clips from incoming mail, we can save rubber bands, and my hope is that we can become awash in those little stretchies also.

Obviously, if we can handle the rubber band challenge, I have something even bigger in mind.

When you are a private enterprise, savings on expenses go to the bottom line. When you are owned by the public, savings still go to the bottom line, but they are in turn magnified by the multiple the stock carries.

If you have trouble understanding the last paragraph, either trust me or call Haimchinkel Malintz Anaynikal directly.

Memo

To   GENERAL & LIMITED PARTNERS Date   September 10, 1985

From   Alan C. Greenberg   CC

Subject **MEMO PADS**

We have been supplying everyone with memo pads. These pads have, at the top, our logo and also a person's name and telephone number. This is conceptually wrong. We are in a person-to-person business. It would be much warmer if the sender of a note signed it with his name and telephone number along with some sweet words, such as "I love you" or "I need more business to feed my family."

Therefore, continuing our goal of trying to increase the income of our associates, pads from now on will only have Bear, Stearns & Co. printed across the top.

It is amazing how one good idea sometimes produces unforeseen benefits. Haimchinkel Malintz Anaynikal just informed me that this superior way of communicating will save us $45,000 a year. What a pleasant surprise!!

Memo

BEAR STEARNS

To   MANAGING &
ASSOCIATE DIRECTORS   Date   December 13, 1985

From   Alan C. Greenberg   CC

Subject

Things are too good!! It is at a time like this that we must be particularly careful, wary, smart, suspicious and, in general, thankful that we are alive. Those of us who have been around for a while know what I mean.

When conditions are this ideal, we are usually being set up for a major unpleasantry. This time around let us try to leave nothing on the table. Times will change, and it will be nice to have plenty of fat on our bones.

Let us continue to watch the shop and realize that none of us are really very smart. We are just in the right place at the right time. Let us continue to watch our expenses like a greenberg so our bottom line looks like a combination of Miss America and Haimchinkel Malintz Anaynikal.

Memo

To   Managing & Associate Directors   Date   January 6, 1986

From   Alan C. Greenberg   CC

Subject

Haimchinkel Malintz Anaynikal was right again. Some of you may have had doubts about his theory on the effects of expense cutting, but the month of December should prove once and for all that the key to profitability is cutting down on the wasteful use of paper clips and rubber bands.

I think December 1985 was the biggest month in the history of Bear Stearns. If we can continue bringing in the business and cutting expenses, the stock may get to 23 1/4.

Now that you are all believers, I would like to see some real effort and results in the expense-cutting area. The rest of our industry cuts expenses when business is bad. We try to cut expenses all the time, but particularly when business is great.

Would we have thought of this brilliant bit of logic without the help of Haimchinkel Malintz Anaynikal? I doubt it, but let us continue to do things differently than others. Our record is pretty good.

Memo

To   MANAGING &
        ASSOCIATE DIRECTORS   Date   February 25, 1986

From   Alan C. Greenberg   CC

Subject

The P&L for the first three months of our public existence is certainly
something to be proud of. Before we fall into one of the traps that
Haimchinkel Malintz Anaynikal so often warned us about, please keep in
mind that we were aided and abetted by a great stock and bond market. I
think it is particularly important that all of us take a little time and review
some fundamentals:

1. We must continue doing our best to control expenses. Every dollar we save
   on expenses goes directly to the bottom line. That is what all of us should
   be concerned about, or you are at the wrong firm. Expenses should be
   watched at all times, but especially when business is good.

2. We must continue to be alert for scams and con artists. We must watch for
   unusual behavior by the people we work with. What is unusual behavior?
   Something subtle like somebody who drives a Rolls-Royce on a salary that
   can barely support roller skates.

3. Do the people you work with answer phone calls in a courteous manner?
   Are all phone calls returned? I couldn't care less what a person does in his
   own home, but I am a nut about returning phone calls that are made to
   our personnel during the workday. I do not care if the caller is selling
   malaria. Calls must be returned!

4. Are the receptionists and telephone operators in all of our offices warm
   and courteous, and if they are, are they thanked appropriately? Remember
   that in most cases the first contact a client has with us is through a
   telephone operator or receptionist.

5. Do you and your associates leave word where you are at all times so that
   finding you is not like hunting for the Andrea Doria?

6. In September of 1983, a memo was distributed with a quote from the
   works of Haimchinkel Malintz Anaynikal. It is worth repeating. "A man
   will do well in commerce as long as he does not believe that his own body
   odor is perfume." That still holds true. We must not get cocky or overconfident.

Remember that the Green Bay Packers won because they executed the
fundamentals better than their competition. Trick plays make headlines,
but winners execute the basics.

Memo

To   MANAGING &
ASSOCIATE DIRECTORS   Date   April 10, 1986

From   ALAN C. GREENBERG   CC

Subject **ERROR ACCOUNT**

It is safe to say that our error account is running at almost 100% efficiency. We have got to do something to stop these insane mistakes, because the loss comes right off the bottom line, and you know how I feel about that particular statistic.

We have been rather cavalier about not charging people for errors. This system obviously has not been working, and when something does not work I believe in change. From this moment on, we reserve the right to debit people who make errors, and this includes managing directors. From this day on, if I or someone who works for me does something stupid, I am going to pay for it. So I would suggest that all of us be careful.

Remember what Haimchinkel Malintz Anaynikal said—"The time to stop stupidity and be tough on costs is when times are good. Any schlemiel* and most schlimazels* try to cut costs when times are bad."

* For those who do not speak Persian, a schlemiel is the one who spills the soup. He spills it on the schlimazel.

Memo

BEAR STEARNS

To	MANAGING & ASSOCIATE DIRECTORS	Date	April 14, 1986
From	Alan C. Greenberg	CC	

Subject **FEDERAL EXPRESS**

This may come as a surprise to some of you, but Federal Express is not a wholly owned subsidiary of Bear, Stearns & Co. Inc. I mention this because we have been spending $50,000 a month with them and there is no explanation to justify this expenditure unless it was an intercompany transfer.

I checked on how much I was charged for Federal Expressing packages to my clients, and the figure for the past 11 months was $68.32. One of those charges was for a package sent to Haimchinkel Malintz Anaynikal. That should be a firm expense, but I am not going to make a big thing out of it. My point is that Federal Express is a luxury, and business can still be done by using the U.S. Mail.

I can assure you that future use of Federal Express is going to be very closely monitored. The fact that it wasn't up to now is my fault, and I take full blame.

After thinking it over, I am going to have Russian reverse that $25 that was charged to me for sending our figures to Haimchinkel Malintz Anaynikal. We must strive for accounting perfection.

Memo

BEAR STEARNS

To   Managing & Associate Directors   Date   April 18, 1986

From   Alan C. Greenberg   CC

Subject **HOW TO GET RICHER**

It is amazing how easy it is to save substantial money when you really put your mind to it. I was dreaming of Haimchinkel Malintz Anaynikal the other night and the following idea came to me.

All of us use blue envelopes for sending written material around the office. Our team has done a great job of saving these envelopes and reusing them, but our scotch tape expense has gone up. From this day on, instruct your secretary to lick only the left side of the flap when sending the envelope. The reason for this will amaze you, and make you wonder why you did not think of this yourself.

If the envelope is gently opened by the recipient, it can be used again and sealed, without using scotch tape, by your secretary licking the right side of the flap and then sealing it.

After all of us have become accustomed to accurate and precise licking, a further extension of this will be to lick only the left third, and then the middle for the next trip, and the right side for the penultimate voyage. If one has a small tongue and good coordination, an envelope could be opened and resealed ten times.

The beauty of this thought is that not only is it practical, but it is 100% sanitary. Our bottom line will continue to grow if all of us can come up with brilliancies similar to this.

Memo

BEAR STEARNS

To: MANAGING & ASSOCIATE DIRECTORS   Date: August 29, 1986

From: Alan C. Greenberg   CC

Subject:

August is now history, but I hated to see it end. The month gave me a great deal of pleasure. The figures are not available yet. They will be excellent but not a new record.

August gave me a charge because I cannot remember a time when all the departments seemed to be working so well. We are really hitting on all cylinders. Frankly, the only negative was our continuing problem of losses due to clerical errors.

Remember what Haimchinkel Malintz Anaynikal once said, "The strength of the strongest chain is determined by its weakest schmuck." It is important that every department of Bear Stearns continue to operate at maximum efficiency.

Congratulations to all of you!

Because we are rolling, it is essential that we review the fundamentals of Haimchinkel Malintz Anaynikal.

1. Reinforce once again with your associates that anything unusual should be brought to the attention of a superior at once. We will never be upset if it is a false alarm.

2. Do not get conceited or cocky.

3. Check on the people who answer telephones. Are they courteous?

4. Return all calls as soon as possible.

5. Watch expenses—like a hawk. Now is the time to cut out fat! The rest of the world cuts expenses when business turns sour. With your help, we will be different, smarter and richer.

6. Reduce expenses.

7. Cut expenses.

8. Do not spend money frivolously. Every dollar we save will go to the bottom line.

Memo

BEAR STEARNS

To   Managing Directors and
Associate Directors

Date   December 9, 1986

From   Alan C. Greenberg

CC

Subject **Getting Richer**

Our growth continues unabated. It is a joy to behold, but when you get busy, I am afraid some leakage does occur. Three examples are detailed below:

1. Telephones not being answered promptly in certain areas. Hire more people! After you hire them, explain to them how important it is that they be courteous and attentive to anyone who calls.

2. This is going to be hard for you to believe, but it is actually a fact. I called the head of one of our major areas yesterday, and although the man was in, his secretary did not know where to find him! I know that this tests my credibility with you, but it is true. You are well aware that this violates one of Haimchinkel Malintz Anaynikal's cardinal rules. I hope HMA* does not hear about this incident.

3. It also hurts me to report that I saw somebody throw away a used envelope before it made 22 trips around the office. I can't stand to see people burn money. Thank goodness I have not seen anyone throwing away rubber bands** or paper clips. Burning money affects our bottom line, and your Executive Committee is judged mainly by one statistic, the bottom line.

Let us all tighten up and reread the 98 memos I have sent out over the past few years.

* This is a clever code for Haimchinkel Malintz Anaynikal.

** Rubber bands can be used even when they break. Take the ends and tie a square knot. If you need to know how to tie a square knot call Bobby Steinberg. He has a cub scout troop consisting only of his sons.

Memo

To	All Managing Directors and Associate Directors	Date	February 5, 1987
From	Alan C. Greenberg	CC	

Subject

I have never been more optimistic about the future of Bear Stearns than I am now. Our third quarter is over and since we are a public company, there is very little I can say about it, but I think that anybody who works here can make a very good guess of how we did. The figures* will be released in late February.

That is only one reason for my optimism. It has become perfectly clear to me that several of our departments have been profitable during the past few years, despite the fact that they were not exactly competing on a "level playing field." Certain competitors have had big advantages over our group; recent events make it clear that this inequity is coming to an end. I congratulate those departments for the job they have done against unethical competition.

You may have also read the articles about a large firm that is deemphasizing arbitraging activities. We at Bear Stearns are actively expanding the personnel and the capital commitments of our risk arbitrage department. I have never been more positive about risk arbitrage. It will amaze me if this decision does not prove correct.

That is the good news. The bad news is we are doing so well that I am sure, subconsciously, we are becoming complacent. It is the job of the Executive Committee to once again stress the fundamentals of Haimchinkel Malintz Anaynikal. You should know what they are by now, and if you do not know, you are at the wrong firm. Because of the tremendous activity in all phases of our business, every con man is or will be heading for the securities industry. Stay alert! And once again reinforce with our associates the need to report anything unusual no matter how trivial.

* Whatever the figures are, they would be even better if my associates read and reread my memos on expenses, but nobody pays attention to me since the stock is above 20.

Memo

BEAR STEARNS

To   Managing Directors
Associate Directors   Date   March 9, 1987

From   Alan C. Greenberg   CC

Subject

It is official! We have signed a lease to move to 46th and Park Avenue. I hope that all of you are as excited about this move as the Executive Committee is. In our opinion, this move ushers in a whole new dimension to our growth.

I would like to take this time to assure you that our basic culture is not going to change. Even though we will have more space and more people, we certainly will not add any additional layers of management. Our point of view on expenses and the bottom line will not change. Our pretax margins were 26.6% for the first 9 months of this year and are the highest in the industry. I am sorry to report that for the same period our return on equity was 25% and ranks only 2nd in the industry. This ranking of our R.O.E. is disappointing to me and particularly to Haimchinkel Malintz Anaynikal. We are obviously doing something wrong. Let us all set about correcting it.

The only statistic I care about is return on equity. After many sessions with some of our business school graduates (yes, we do have some), I think they have helped me understand the secret to improving our R.O.E. It seems that if we increase revenues and cut expenses, return on equity goes up and that is what makes me happy. Please make me happy! I can be very unpleasant when I'm not.

Memo

BEAR STEARNS

To   **ALL EMPLOYEES**   Date   April 30, 1987

From   Alan C. Greenberg   CC

Subject **PHONE MANNER**

This girl must have read some of our memos. Please read what she has to say and let us try to implement it in every nook and cranny of Bear Stearns.

'Phone doctor' has an Rx for telerudeness

By Cindy Richards

The federal budget deficit, international trade gap and unstable stock market may grab the headlines, but Nancy Friedman says the biggest problem facing business today is rudeness.

"The sales department just bleeds when people are treated badly," said Friedman, who bills herself as the Telephone Doctor.

In seminars conducted for companies across the country, Friedman teaches employees to be nice to folks on the phone.

"I don't know that we're showing anybody anything terribly new," Friedman said in a telephone interview last week. But, she noted, just because employees know they should treat callers well doesn't mean they're doing it.

Take "emotional leakage," for example. That's when the employee is upset about something else and takes it out on the caller. Before answering the phone in a bad mood, Friedman suggests letting it ring one more time— long enough to dredge up a smile. "A phony smile is better than a real frown," the energetic Friedman says.

Then there are Friedman's "five forbidden phrases."

- *"I don't know."* It should be replaced with "Let me check and find out."
- *"We can't do that."* Instead, tell callers what can be done.
- *"You'll have to . . ."* The caller doesn't have to do much of anything, certainly not sit on hold. Instead, the employee should say, "You'll need to . . ."
- *"Hang on a second, I'll be right back."* It's a lie and should be replaced with "I'll need to put you on hold for a few moments, if you are able to hold."
- *"No."* It should no longer appear at the beginning of a sentence. That makes people think about what they're saying before they start talking.

To Friedman, polite use of the telephone is not just a business, it's a crusade. In her quest to stamp out phone rudeness, she is offering a supply of "telephone violation" and "telephone commendation" notices free to anyone. The notices are to be sent to the boss of the person to be reprimanded or commanded. They may be obtained by writing the Telephone Doctor, P.O. Box 777, St. Louis, Mo. 63044.

(from the Chicago Sun-Times)

Memo

To   MANAGING DIRECTORS
AND ASSOCIATE DIRECTORS   Date   May 26, 1987

From   ALAN C. GREENBERG   CC

Subject

The cover story in last week's Time Magazine was on ethics. Most of what they said was nonsense, but the magazine did make a point of saying that one of the problems of detecting fraud or "nauties" in corporations is that employees of most companies are afraid to rock the boat by reporting aberrations or suspicious actions.

I think that it is time once again to stress that we think all of our people are honest, and they are even more honest when they (including the members of the Executive Committee) know they are being watched like a hawk by everyone in our organization. As you know, we even reward people with cash bonuses if a suspicion is substantiated.

Let us restate to our associates that they are our first line of defense against fraud and waste. We need their cooperation to stay pure, and we will reward them if they discover an indiscretion. We will also never criticize anyone for calling "wolf" too often.

We are different from other corporations. Let us stay that way.

Memo

BEAR STEARNS

TO: Managing Directors
Associate Directors

DATE: June 18, 1987

FROM: Alan C. Greenberg

The more you read about our competitors' problems, the more you realize what a job our people did in the month of April.

The media are consistent. They seem to print only negatives about Bear Stearns. Our earnings for the year and quarter ending April 30, 1987 were given to the newspapers, and we stressed in our release that the month of April was plenty volatile, but we did fine.

It is hard not to get upset when you see our stock behave as it has, but I can assure you that if our record continues, our multiple will increase dramatically. My guarantee may not mean much, but Haimchinkel Malintz Anaynikal agrees, and that does mean something.

If we continue to earn 50% on our equity (pre-tax), some MBA will recognize us, and then we may even sell at nine times earnings.

We are doing great! Just keep it up and leave the price of the stock to me.

Memo

To	ALL MANAGING DIRECTORS	Date	July 13, 1987
From	THE EXECUTIVE COMMITTEE	CC	

Subject COST CONTROL AND OVERALL EFFICIENCY

Bear Stearns has recently announced a record year—a period during which some of the majors in our industry had problems in certain areas that affected adversely their P&L. We may be entitled to some degree of pride in our performance, but certainly not smug self-satisfaction.

While our cost/revenue ratios appear to be reasonably satisfactory, now is the time to pause and remind ourselves that:

1) We have expanded rapidly, adding 800 employees during FY 1987 alone;

2) The move to 245 Park Avenue will increase significantly our fixed expenses;

3) Our industry is cyclical, and we are in the midst of the longest bull market in history;

4) A sharp downturn could be painful if we are not lean and mean;

5) Many of us get paid primarily out of bonus pool profits; and,

6) Inevitably fat creeps in with expansion and prosperity.

Consequently, we want all Managing Directors to begin critically examining their areas. Here is a list of some of the things you should be reviewing:

A. Your work force

1. Who is not sufficiently productive?

2. Who should be replaced?

continued . . .

Memo

3. Who should be eliminated and need not be replaced?

4. Before hiring anyone new, ask whether your existing staff can be assigned additional responsibilities.

5. Do you have employees performing functions that are duplicating those performed in other departments, such as Accounting or Data Processing?

B. Other items to watch and do that will keep us neat & clean.

1. Are you paying for unused or uneconomic news or quotation services?

2. Are you paying outside vendors for services or material that are not really needed, or duplicate what is already available in-house?

3. Do you have too many telephones and underutilized fixed wires?

4. Are you controlling such things as Federal Express, messenger services, and personal long-distance calls?

5. Do you & your associates reread daily my major memos on rubber bands, paper clips and envelope recycling (I feel that adhering to those memos was the main reason last year was a success).

Bear Stearns has grown and prospered because capable, aggressive, money-motivated people worked hard, were given substantial responsibility, and watched their businesses and each other. The biggest challenge is yet to come—start getting ready NOW.

If you don't do it—we will have to do it for you and that will be less pleasant and less efficient. This place is not going to smell like a bureaucracy—bureaucracies don't set records. We own 60% of this place—let's keep it sound and make it grow. Our compensation is based on the firm's profitability. In addition, I am newly married, and I am in no mood to take a pay cut. Regardless of what your experience has been, I am finding that two cannot live as cheaply as one.

Memo

BEAR STEARNS

To   MANAGING DIRECTORS AND
      <u>ASSOCIATE DIRECTORS</u>   Date   August 21, 1987

From   ALAN C. GREENBERG   CC

Subject

Bear Stearns is <u>not having a hiring freeze</u>. Our experience has been that the best time to hire productive people is when conditions are difficult. Some areas of Wall Street are having problems and that means opportunity is once again knocking at our door. Let us all be alert and continue to build!

I would like to announce at this time a freeze on expenses and carelessness. We probably throw away millions every year with stupidities and slop. In fact, I have seen more slop in the last three weeks than in the previous six months. Stop it now. No business is strong enough to withstand constant stupidity.

Haimchinkel Malintz Anaynikal is really something. Just take a look at my June 13, 1987 memo and see once again how right he was. He hates slop, even more than I do. In fact, he pointed out to me where our stock could be if we ran a neat, tight shop. I am tired of cleaning up poo-poos. The next associate of mine that does something "un-neat" is going to have a little meeting with me and I will not be the usual charming, sweet, understanding, pleasant, entertaining, affable yokel from Oklahoma.

Memo

To   <u>MANAGING DIRECTORS</u>
     <u>ASSOCIATE DIRECTORS</u>

Date   October 16, 1987

From   ALAN C. GREENBERG

CC

Subject

Over the years Haimchinkel Malintz Anaynikal has stressed:

1. Hire PSD's.*

2. Make decisions based on common sense and avoid the herd mentality.

3. Control expenses with unrelenting vigil, because if you turn your back for a second they will grow like weeds.

4. Help all departments to grow, because this year's starlet can be next year's dog.

5. Beware of catchy phrases—such as "Merchant Banking." Haimchinkel Malintz Anaynikal knew I was not clear on what Merchant Banking is, so he defined it for me.

   "Merchant Banking is buying stock in a company whose shares are not publicly traded and the company should be in a business very different from what you are familiar with."

   Imagine, all this time I thought Merchant Banking was some esoteric, complicated British secret.

Haimchinkel Malintz Anaynikal's guides may seem simplistic, but why don't we give them a try?

* For those of you who are new to Bear Stearns, PSD stands for poor, smart and a deep desire to become rich. Please do not infer from this that Haimchinkel Malintz Anaynikal is prejudiced against people who possess other almost worthless degrees. He is not nor does he teach others to be.

Memo

BEAR STEARNS

To	MANAGING & ASSOCIATE DIRECTORS	Date	October 19, 1987
From	ALAN C. GREENBERG	CC	

Subject

It is amazing how history keeps repeating itself. The market in stocks and bonds has taken a precipitous drop, but I am far from depressed. Why? Because once again we are seeing and we will be seeing great opportunities in all areas, particularly in personnel. I can assure you we are pursuing every lead at this very moment.

Our move to Park Avenue will start shortly, and I truly believe that the timing is perfect. Just keep in mind it was just a few years ago that two of our competitors left the clearing business. Eleven months ago several large firms closed their Arbitrage Departments.* We will be a <u>winner</u>.

A market like this does bring out the worst in people. The enclosed vicious rumor was sent to the media last week. Your Executive Committee knew immediately that it was false, because Haimchinkel Malintz Anaynikal certainly would have left a huge number of rubber bands and old envelopes in his estate. It is logical, quick thinking like this by your leaders that ensures our firm's success.

* I wish our Arbitrage Department had closed down for a two-week fall vacation fourteen days ago.

HAIMCHINKEL M. ANAYNIKAL DIES
OF ACUTE OVEREXPOSURE

New York, N.Y.—Mr. Haimchinkel Malintz Anaynikal died last night —a victim of acute overexposure.

The controversial Bear Stearns consultant is survived by his former wife, from whom he was divorced the day after his marriage thirty years ago. "That tightwad wanted me to pay half the hotel bill on our honeymoon," she lamented.

Mr. Anaynikal left an estate of 5,475,000 paper clips, and a gigantic ball of string, which almost completely occupied a bedroom in his sparse loft apartment.

Acting as the sole honorary pallbearer, and the only mourner at his funeral, was Bear Stearns chairman Alan "Ace" Greenberg. Mr. Greenberg, sobbing uncontrollably, could only say, "I can't believe Haimchinkel is dead. What will become of me. I don't know how I can go on without him."

Memo

To   ALL REGISTERED
REPRESENTATIVES   Date   November 3, 1987

From   ALAN C. GREENBERG   CC

Subject

Enclosed is a memo that Kathryn Estey of the Chicago office sent to me. It was dictated by me and distributed in July of 1984. When you read it, you'll realize how times have changed. The one thing that hasn't changed is the services that I hope all Registered Representatives get from the staff.

These have been tough times for the Operations Department, but things are getting back to normal and I still want you to feel free to call me anytime you feel the service is less than Triple A.

We have come through a tough period, but believe me, your firm is stronger now in terms of personnel than it was one month ago, and we are still growing.

Memo

BEAR STEARNS

To	Managing Directors and Associate Directors	Date	November 16, 1987
From	ALAN C. GREENBERG	CC	

Subject

Our second quarter just ended and the results are a matter of record. The month of October will never be forgotten by any of us or by historians.

The pressure was tremendous on everyone who had anything to do with equities, and in almost every case our people came through beautifully. I would like to thank them all personally, but that is impossible. But it is possible for you to do it for me. Please let the people you work with know how I feel about them.

The firm weathered the storm almost unscathed, but our stockholders were hurt not only by the 32% drop in the stock market but also by the withdrawal of the Jardine offer—a double disappointment. It is our job to make the month of October look in retrospect like a blessing in disguise for Bear Stearns. I know this appears to be a tough assignment, but we are making the moves now that make this possible. We will do it!

The Jardine cancellation affected me in a different way. Haimchinkel Malintz Anaynikal suggested and I agreed to drop out of my grouse-shooting class. It just was not me. I took one lesson and the only thing I learned was that the plural of grouse is greese. Haimchinkel Malintz Anaynikal failed to see how that kind of knowledge would now be of great aid to my career.

BEAR STEARNS

To	Managing Directors Associate Directors	Date	November 24, 1987
From	ALAN C. GREENBERG	CC	
Subject			

The move of the New York Office has started!

If you have not seen the interior of 245 Park Avenue yet, you have a real treat in store. The Corporate Finance and M&A Departments are now in operation at 46th and Park. The rest of us will be moving shortly, and I truly believe that our timing is perfect.

The newspapers have been full of news about layoffs in every area of our industry, and there will be plenty of additional fallout if E.F. Hutton is taken over by another Wall Street firm. We now have the space and the appetite to hire people if they have outstanding ability. Our new location will make us an even more desirable place to work.

Why are we hiring instead of firing? Maybe it is because we followed the teachings of Haimchinkel Malintz Anaynikal when others scoffed. Rather than test fate, your Executive Committee has agreed to go along with Haimchinkel Malintz Anaynikal's latest suggestion. Because of our past growth and our anticipated growth, we have reluctantly decided to adapt some modern management techniques suggested by Haimchinkel Malintz Anaynikal.

We will shortly set up a group devoted only to <u>Backward Planning</u>. This may surprise some of you, but look deeper and you will discover the logic behind this move. Just examine the records of those companies that had personnel devoted to strategic or forward planning, and you will figure out this initial plunge by us into a more structured corporate environment.

The composition of this group has not been finalized, but such things as not returning telephone calls, having a secretary who answers calls with the enthusiasm of a wet noodle, being late to client meetings and just being "not neat and tidy" certainly are the things we will be looking for in a candidate for the Backward Planning Committee.

Memo

BEAR
STEARNS

To   All Directors of Bear Stearns
Managing Directors and
Associate Directors   Date   February 3, 1988

From   Alan C. Greenberg   CC

Subject

Our move to Park Avenue is almost complete. As far as I am concerned, it went like a dream and the first month (January) was a real pleasure.

If January is any indication of the future, we are going to have some real fun.

Firms in our industry continue to be shaken by internal problems* and we remain free from this poison. One of the main jobs of your Executive Committee is to keep it that way. The firm is riding high now and everyone who works here can feel it (we are hiring—they are firing). Haimchinkel Malintz Anaynikal has warned us once again that the only thing that can stop our momentum is internal strife, conceit and complacency. We will not let it happen at Bear Stearns! We have come too far to turn stupid.

Everybody's doing great. Keep it up and make me richer.

* It was just announced that some prominent people in M&A just left a firm because of a difference of opinion over strategic planning. An issue like that could never arise at Bear Stearns because we have no strategic planning. Once again, Haimchinkel Malintz Anaynikal comes out as one smart dude. Remember his Axiom 1023? "The amount of dissension rises geometrically with the more issues you have to philosophize over."

Memo

To	All Senior Managing Directors, Managing Directors, and Associate Directors	Date	April 12, 1988
From	Alan C. Greenberg	CC	

Subject

In two weeks our fiscal year will end, but I can assure you the memory will linger on.

It was a year that made us realize how fragile the markets can be and that we can never lower our guard.

The year also showed us how expensive litigation can be—even when we are right! What is the answer? We must be careful, suspicious and always respect our in-house administrators and compliance people. It is impossible to make enough on a trade or a deal to justify subsequent litigation due to carelessness or greed.

The positives of last year were many. We showed remarkable composure and the ability to rebound under pressure. Every department used October 19, 1987 as an opportunity to attract top people. We are the only investment banking firm I know of that is hiring and not firing (5,715 employees a year ago versus 6,036 today). This has caused the morale of our associates to be at an all-time high. The year also showed our tremendous earning power even when the market had a record break.

I do have one sad item to report. Haimchinkel Malintz Anaynikal will no longer serve as a consultant on a regular basis. After ten years of my badgering him, he is just plain tired; but we will not be wholly on our own. He will be available for special problems, and we will be able to talk to his nephew, Itzhak Nanook* Pumpernickanaylian, on mundane subjects.

The bottom line is I have never felt more optimistic about our future or more eager to come to work in the morning. I hope you feel the same.

* Remember, Haimchinkel Malintz Anaynikal's mother was an Eskimo.

Memo

To   All Employees   Date   April 15, 1988

From   Alan C. Greenberg   CC

Subject

Itzhak Nanook Pumpernickanaylian is in harness and running, and
he has come up with his first brilliancy.

While going through our new quarters (he was on a camel), he pointed
out to me that we have 2,600 pieces of returned mail sitting in a
room at 245 Park Avenue. Why is this? These pieces of mail, some of
which may be very important, were returned to us because of wrong
addresses, but the senders did not put any identification in the upper
left-hand corner of the envelopes. At this time we have been unable to
find the senders. We have retained Sherlock Schwartz, but this case
is too much even for him.

Effective today we have a new policy. In fact, we should have had
it for the past 10 years. Nothing goes out of Bear Stearns without
the sender's identifying mark in the upper left-hand corner of each
envelope. This will save us time, money and aggravation. If you are
too busy to do this, please call me. I will be glad to come down and
put the proper identification on your mail.

1988–1991

October of 1987 was a tough month, but the three and a half years that followed were a real test of the viability of a firm in the brokerage industry. Four prominent firms (L.F. Rothschild, Drexel Burnham Lambert, Thomson McKinnon and E.F. Hutton) disappeared, and four equally prominent houses would have exited if their parents had not come to the rescue with $3½ billion. Three and a half billion dollars—the figure is mind-boggling.

During that period Bear Stearns continued to prosper, and we believe we are now in the strongest position in our history—strong financially and strong in all areas in which we compete.

How did we resist some of the wild things our competitors were doing that made real inroads into our market share? How did we keep our associates in place when transactions they brought in were lost to other firms that were willing to do things we were not willing to do? How and why did we resist the bridge loan mania? It was not easy. At times we were questioned by our own people as to whether we were out of touch with the real world. And there were occasions when even we doubted the principles we so stubbornly maintained. Maybe these memos can give you some insight on how we managed to keep our equilibrium, and in so doing, how we managed to greatly improve our position in our industry.

All of us at Bear Stearns are looking forward to the future. We think we are poised to make an even bigger impact in the world of finance.

BEAR STEARNS

M E M O

To	Senior Managing Directors Managing Directors Associate Directors	Date	June 20, 1988
From	**ALAN C. GREENBERG**	CC	

Subject

Itzhak Nanook Pumpernickanaylian (his mother calls him Nookie*) has observed that our new fiscal year did not exactly start during a very impressive month for our industry.

My guess is that we are doing better than most of our competitors, but that does not make me happy. Nookie's only advice was to implore all of us to work harder. Conditions do change quickly in this business, and if we are doing okay when things are tough, we will break records when the market turns.

Nookie also made the comment that "the harder you work, the luckier you get." This thought is neither original nor new, but it is true and we can all use luck.

Keep your chins up, we are going in the right direction.

* Haimchinkel Malintz Anaynikal tried to explain to Mrs. Pumpernickanaylian that Nookie was not considered a particularly flattering nickname in some circles; so she started calling her son Nofkee. Haimchinkel immediately asked her to switch back to Nookie.

To   Senior Managing Directors
Managing Directors
Associate Directors   Date   August 30, 1988

From   Alan C. Greenberg   CC

Subject

Nookie sent a message to us that may sound trite but still bears repeating.

"The business you are in is just plain difficult at this time. When you entered the industry, you were warned that it was cyclical but bull markets tend to cloud realism. You are now in a period that separates the men from the boys.

Mrs. Haimchinkel Malintz Anaynikal suggests that when the going gets tough—go shopping!

A certain officer of Bear Stearns suggests that when the going gets tough—start selling positions!

My suggestion is that when the going gets tough—the tough get going!

You have no option but to follow my suggestion. If you do, you will prosper beyond your wildest dreams when the market turns— and it will.

> Your advisor, junior grade
> Itzhak Nanook
> Pumpernickanaylian"

There is not much to add. We will be one of the survivors and the people that stick with us will prosper mightily. The next bull market could start any day and the strong will still be here for the fun.

BEAR STEARNS

M E M O

To	All Senior Managing Directors	Date	October 4, 1988
From	Alan C. Greenberg	CC	

Subject A Field Report from Itzhak Nanook Pumpernickanaylian

Haimchinkel Malintz Anaynikal hosted a family gathering on October 3rd. This is an annual party celebrating the most important of all Eskimo holidays (remember, Haimchinkel Malintz Anaynikal's mother was an Eskimo). It was 82 years ago that the Eskimo Pie was invented, so you can see why people up north rank this day just ahead of the feast celebrating the invention of the harpoon.*

It is reported to me by Nookie that Haimchinkel Malintz Anaynikal is very optimistic on Wall Street. Why? Because he pointed out that big money is usually made by contrarians and at the moment the world is down on our industry.

If you think back, you will discover that our best moves were made against the thinking of the masses. I truly believe that now is the time to enter the securities business—not the time to leave—but it is up to us to be leaders. It is not easy to be up when your area of the industry is down 50%, but it will turn and we must and will help the weak survive this period.

It is incumbent upon us that we keep our people from thinking the grass is greener somewhere else. It is incumbent upon us to recognize who needs help. It is incumbent upon us to stress that the contrarian point of view is the intelligent course.

The bottom line is: there is no substitute for leadership. Now is the time to demonstrate what I know we have.

* Some of the young male Moes (short for Eskimos) particularly like the Feast of Harpoon because for a 24-hour period you are allowed to spear anything in sight.

BEAR STEARNS

M E M O

To
Sr. Managing Directors
Managing Directors
Associate Directors

Date   October 26, 1988

From   Alan C. Greenberg

CC

Subject

Electricity is not free! This will come as a complete surprise to 98% of the people who work at Bear Stearns. Why am I so sure? Nookie* took a little walk around our offices one evening and found enough lights and machines on to fund Bangladesh's light bill for a year.

I have never enjoyed the smell of money burning, particularly when it is my money. The careless wasting of electricity is burning money. (Our electrical bill is running at the rate of five million a year.)

From this day on we have two revolutionary new rules. Turn off lights when you leave a room and turn off equipment when you call it a day. With concentration, dedication and muscular coordination we can do it! Nookie* suggested we hire a therapist to help our associates handle this major job adjustment, but I think he underestimates our people. Prove me right or it is off to therapy sessions.

* If you do not know who Nookie is by now, you are at the wrong firm.

BEAR
STEARNS

M E M O

To
Senior Managing Directors
Managing Directors
Associate Directors

Date   November 9, 1988

From   Alan C. Greenberg

CC

Subject

October was an excellent month, and November is starting off great. I think my memo about turning off lights had a lot to do with the profitability of the last forty days. Our profits would have been even higher if our people had responded with more enthusiasm to my requests about cutting down our electrical bill.

I will take part of the blame for lack of total compliance because I did not realize the complexities involved. Our staff did well in turning off switches that were on a vertical plane, but switches that were on a horizontal plane seemed to cause major problems.

Nookie* explained the reason for this to me. Although most of us are P.S.D.'s,* we still live in homes with electricity and the switches for room lights are on the walls, not the <u>floors</u>. Please file this fact. Our associates performed miserably in turning off the electronic machines. Can you figure out why? Nookie knew at once. Let me help you. All the switches for these apparatuses are on a <u>horizontal plane</u>. Our group could not adjust! Please have seminars in your areas explaining how these switches work. Our alternative is to have the switches on all the machines changed to a vertical position. This would cost $8,492,212.00. Your Executive Committee thinks with your help our staff can adjust.

I cannot stand to see our money being burnt. Stop all waste!

* If you do not know who Nookie is or what a P.S.D. is, do not read any further. You will never understand the text that follows.

	Senior Managing Directors		
	Managing Directors		
To	Associate Directors	Date	December 20, 1988

| From | Alan C. Greenberg | CC | |

Subject

We are going through one of those periods. Some departments are breaking records and it appears that everything they touch turns to gold. We have been around long enough to know two things.

1. Every cat house has its night. Those departments that are having problems at the moment will have their day in the sun, but until then our job is to keep morale up and the people in place.

2. Those areas that are coining money will have a tendency to get overconfident and a little loose and/or forgetful of the fundamentals that built this place.

That is where our P.S.D. degrees come into play. We are going to stress, reinforce and become just plain obnoxious about stopping overconfidence and conceit. When the party ends in these hot areas, I do not want the Executive Committee to have to do clean-up duty. We must keep our associates' feet on the ground. The party will end and I want to give back the absolute minimum.

Our second quarter will be over in a week and I thank all of you for a lovely Christmas present. I will say no more.

Hope 1989 is good to all of us!

BEAR STEARNS

M E M O

<table>
<tr><td>To</td><td>Senior Managing Directors
Managing Directors
Associate Directors</td><td>Date</td><td>January 13, 1989</td></tr>
<tr><td>From</td><td>Alan C. Greenberg</td><td>CC</td><td></td></tr>
</table>

Subject

You have all seen the results of the last quarter and I must admit they were spectacular considering the present environment.

The Press does not know how sensational the month of December was. A golfer would call the month "a double eagle." We have had big months in the past and they were always the result of all departments contributing. The results of December were achieved with many departments **not** contributing because of industry conditions beyond their control.

Nookie thinks that the business could have an upturn and when that happens I can only dream of the joy in store for us.

A negative note that continues to show its ugly head is that our Error Account continues on its merry way. We had one big hit last week and one very close call that missed us only because of luck— not brains. Once again we have to emphasize to everyone on our payroll that systems and procedures are better than nothing but there is no substitute for using one's head.

Please reemphasize that we reward on the spot people who show brains with cash and/or a promotion when they use their heads.

One of Nookie's main tenets is that "fish stink from the head." If the management gives the appearance of being alert and suspicious, the people under you will act accordingly; so our task is simple. Be smart, act smart, be alert, be suspicious, and on guard!

The only thing that can stop us from getting richer is stupidity.

BEAR STEARNS

M E M O

To	Sr. Managing Directors Managing Directors Associate Directors	Date	April 7, 1989
From	Alan C. Greenberg	CC	

Subject

We have had a policy for years with regard to any of us at Bear Stearns talking to the press.

The rule is simple. No one is allowed to talk on or off the record without the approval of Jim Cayne or John Rosenwald. When I say no one I mean it, because I respect this rule and if I do, you <u>will</u>. This rule obviously includes letting your name appear in any business-related article or advertisement. Please be sure that everybody you work with understands this loud and clear.

As long as we are discussing vocal cords, Itzhak Nanook Pumpernickanaylian pointed out to me that I should also stress our policy on discussing what other firms in our industry do. We <u>do not</u> knock the pricing or the structure of the offerings of our competitors. I am well aware that other firms have not been so considerate toward us, but that has no bearing on how we conduct ourselves.

Our record of late will probably create some jealousy, so it is more important than ever that we conduct ourselves in a manner beyond reproach.

Nookie also made a few comments in general about Bear Stearns. Nookie feels that the morale and spirit at Bear Stearns has never been better, and the future has never looked brighter. I agree most emphatically. Nookie disclosed that he based his conclusions on spot interviews and personal observations. If you are very observant, you may have noticed somebody in Arab garb walking around the premises constantly licking an eskimo pie* and using a walrus phallus* for a toothpick. You keen ones may have guessed it—that was Nookie in his spy outfit.

* You new associates may not be aware of Nookie's heritage. On his mother's maternal side, his grandmother was an Eskimo and his grandfather was an Iranian.

M E M O

	Sr. Managing Directors		
	Managing Directors		
To	Associate Directors	Date	April 18, 1989
From	Alan C. Greenberg	CC	

Subject

Some time ago we informed the people at Bear Stearns that no legal business, printing business, plumbing business or anything else that Bear Stearns pays for can be assigned without the approval of David Glaser (x3763) or Richard De Rose (x3767).

I made a terrible mistake. I did not remind you of this every three months as I should have; so I am reminding you now. If you bite a dog and need a lawyer, you can hire one without our permission. If you expect Bear Stearns to pay a legal bill, you had better get the permission of one of these men I mentioned or you will end up paying the bill yourself.

	Senior Managing Directors		
	Managing Directors		
To	Associate Directors	Date	May 9, 1989
From	Alan C. Greenberg	CC	

Subject

The media have been full of articles about Wall Street and the problems of our industry. The writers quote the same sages they have in the past. The articles fail to mention the prophetical record of these luminaries—their record is lousy.

It was just a short time ago that we were told a Wall Street firm had to be part of a huge financial colossus (Equitable, Metropolitan, Prudential, Sears, etc.) to survive. We are now being told that it is the boutiques that will prosper.

Nookie Pookie* thinks that our structure is perfect and I agree. Firms with an extensive retail branch system will have a headache for many years, but our style of having only six domestic branches with in-house capability in many areas is proving to be the wise way to incorporate retail into the system. We are <u>totally committed</u> to the retail business, but in <u>our way</u>. All of our offices and departments, including retail, are poised to make major contributions to our profitability.

Our record of late is not an accident. When the markets turn optimistic and volume returns, we will set new records in the area I like—net after taxes.

Nookie Pookie* did point out one thing the wire houses have that we should try to buy—their P/E multiples.

* This is the affectionate way he is addressed by his wife, Pastrami.

MEMO

To	Senior Managing Directors Managing Directors Associate Directors	Date	June 9, 1989
From	Alan C. Greenberg	CC	

Subject

I had a dream. The dream was that I returned to this world as a seller of fax machines and I had Bear Stearns as an account. We are ordering fax machines around here like they are being given away—and they are not!

We had a study done of fax machines and it has been proven conclusively that the machines do not object to different people using them. This means that it is possible for people and departments to share in the use of these <u>inanimate</u> objects.

Before you or your associates request another machine, please explore sharing or moving a machine we already own closer to your area.

This idea is a good one and I can say that because it was not mine. It came from Nookie's wife* and sister-in-law. Common sense seems to flow in the veins of that group.

* You remember his wife Pastrami. She is half of the famous Meeskeit twins—Salami and Pastrami. The Meeskeit twins were considered their culture's answer to the Gabors.

BEAR
STEARNS

M E M O

To ALL 245 PARK AVE., 866 U.N. PLAZA
and 2 BROADWAY EMPLOYEES

Date June 15, 1989

From Alan C. Greenberg

CC

Subject CALLING THE OPERATOR INSTEAD OF USING THE DIRECTORY

Itzhak Nanook Pumpernickanaylian just completed a survey to determine why we can't answer the main number (212-272-2000) in less than two rings during the peak periods in a day.

Guess what! Nookie pointed out that over 50% of all calls are coming in from our own people (from inside the building). Instead of looking the number up in the directory, people simply call the operator. Let me remind everyone that while it may seem a little more convenient to call the operator, it is also impacting the way we handle the customers of the firm. We should be giving the best service to people who may give us business.

Nookie suggests that you start using your brain and stop using the operators as a directory!

BEAR STEARNS

To	Senior Managing Directors Managing Directors Associate Directors	Date	June 30, 1989
From	Alan C. Greenberg	CC	

Subject

Our year ended on June 30th. I would say the last three months were bogey, par, eagle! It always feels good to end on an up-tick and June was a pleasure.

It would be inappropriate for me to comment on the specific profitability of the quarter (smile, giggle) but the results will be public knowledge very soon. It started off slow, but then we got lucky—this was our 44th lucky quarter in a row!

All of us who work here can feel the excitement and spirit that this firm is generating. Nookie* conducted a confidential survey at Bear Stearns and concluded that, on a scale of 1 to 10, the morale of our people is a 12.

Some of the decisions we have made since October 1987 are really paying off. Two of the best were "hiring instead of firing" and expanding departments that other firms were closing or contracting. These departments are or are on the verge of making major contributions!

The past year on an absolute basis was great, but on a relative basis it was spectacular. If we stick to the fundamentals (my next six memos will cover that subject) and keep our momentum going, we will break all records.

I have just learned that a bank in southern Alabama has bought 2,200 shares of Bear Stearns common stock. The synergism that this association could generate is mind-boggling. How could you be anything but wildly optimistic on our future?

* Do you remember being queried by a little man in a polar bear coat, galoshes and wearing a pith helmet? You guessed it, that was Nookie in his camouflage interview outfit.

To	Sr. Managing Directors Managing Directors Associate Directors	Date	July 17, 1989
From	Alan C. Greenberg	CC	

Subject

The in-house telephone operators are being swamped by our own associates dialing the Bear Stearns operator and asking to be connected to another Bear Stearns employee. All of us have been given Bear Stearns directories and we should dial the numbers ourselves. This will free up our operators to do constructive things like adequately servicing clients who are trying to reach our switchboard.

There are two reasons that the directories are not being used:
1. Laziness
2. Not being able to read

Nookie has suggested ways to handle both possibilities. The chief operator will keep a record of employees who need constant help from the operators. If those people are literate, they will meet with me.

For those associates who cannot read, we will have people on every floor with the designation of H.I.* If someone needs help in reading the directory, all they have to do is yell "HI" and help will arrive. This will not only improve our service, but could also increase the social life of the dumbbells.

This format should kill every cat in the alley.

* Code name for Helper of Illiterates.

To
SENIOR MANAGING DIRECTORS
MANAGING DIRECTORS
ASSOCIATE DIRECTORS

Date   SEPTEMBER 19, 1989

From   ALAN C. GREENBERG

CC

Subject

Some time ago Itzhak Nanook Pumpernickanaylian physically restrained me from releasing a memo I had written about the increase of careless, expensive errors that were popping up throughout the firm. The errors ran the gamut from failing to cancel good-till-cancel orders to entering a buy order when it should be a sell order. The people involved represent a cross section of the firm—from clerks to senior managing directors.

Nookie's reasoning was that in the past every time we brought up the subject of errors and penalties, our people became so nervous that errors increased.

The stock market has not been extremely active or frantic lately, but the error situation has turned critical during the last month. The size and frequency of the errors would put a dent in the U.S. Mint; so obviously it is a luxury we cannot afford.

From this day on we will use new tools to combat this stupidity. Please inform the people you work with that restitution will be the mildest penalty. Every error will be shown to the Executive Committee, and they will take appropriate action. We must stop this intrusion of our bottom line.

BEAR STEARNS

M E M O

To	SENIOR MANAGING DIRECTORS MANAGING DIRECTORS ASSOCIATE DIRECTORS	Date	OCTOBER 2, 1989
From	ALAN C. GREENBERG	CC	

Subject

Would you pay $72 for something you could buy for $10?

Our internal auditors have documented 44 instances in the past year where departments purchased a total of 1,356 rolls of FAX paper directly from vendors for prices ranging from $10 to $72 per roll. The purchases were authorized by 28 different people, including eight SMDs and one member of the executive committee.

We have a Purchasing Department, delighted to deliver FAX paper to you for $7.35 per roll. Why not call them?

We are offering an incentive to induce you to use Purchasing. In the future, accounts payable will not pay any invoice (over $200) for equipment or supplies without Purchasing Department's approval. If Purchasing finds it could have obtained the item at a lower price, the Senior Managing Director or other executive who authorized the purchase will be charged personally for the difference.

You can obtain prompt advance price quotes from Purchasing by calling Yvonne Abbott (x8774).

Some of you may have wondered why we have a department called Purchasing. This memo should answer your questions. The purpose of this department is to purchase supplies and items for all of us at Bear Stearns. Either use that department or pay. Enough is enough.

	Senior Managing Directors		
	Managing Directors		
To	Associate Directors	Date	November 9, 1989
From	Alan C. Greenberg	CC	

Subject

Here we go again. Business is tough. The Dow Jones index dropped almost 200 points a month ago. Firms are announcing major layoffs.

What is our posture at this time? Your executive committee feels we should be <u>hiring, not firing</u>. This is the time to pick up great people. This position may amaze some newer associates, but those of you who have been exposed to our culture will not be surprised by this move. Being a contrarian has worked for us in the past and it will work again.

Spread the word—<u>we are hiring, not firing</u>. The flip side is that our associates should be relieved and maybe the people who work here will even appreciate what a great place this is to build a career.

Nookie points out that we have been remiss in not blowing our own horn a little louder. It amazes him that we have lost people to firms that expand and then contract like accordions. Being bashful was cute in Snow White; Nookie sees nothing wrong in exposing our people to the hiring and firing records of our competitors.

One of the biggest payers of up-front money to registered representatives went out of the retail business after causing us three years of grief. This was not an isolated incident. We have to help our people look beyond their noses.

To	Senior Managing Directors Managing Directors Associate Directors	Date	December 20, 1989
From	Alan C. Greenberg	CC	

Subject

You may have received a notice that the fixed income area in New York was holding an auction on December 19th for the benefit of Ann Carnes' grandchildren. Ann works for us on the floor of the New York Stock Exchange and her grandchildren lost their father a short time ago. The auction and donations raised about $150,000! Every member of Bear Stearns should feel proud of this outpouring for an associate.

You have probably also heard that Moodys just **raised** the rating of our senior debt and preferred stock. Calling this a positive in this current Wall Street atmosphere is an understatement.

When you couple those events with the fact that we are hiring, not firing, maybe you can understand why the morale at Bear Stearns is, and should be, as high as it is.

This is a rough period, but your Executive Committee is determined to make it work to our advantage. We are going to come out of this stronger and we will be competing in a smaller universe.

Have a great holiday and I hope you are looking forward to 1990 as much as I am. We are on the right track and you are at the right place—spread the word.

To	Senior Managing Directors Managing Directors Associate Directors	Date	January 22, 1990
From	Alan C. Greenberg	CC	

Subject

Our earnings for the quarter and first six months of our fiscal year were released last Thursday. They would have been much better if we were not the biggest buyer of FAX machines in the western world. My opinion of the quarter was that it was O.K. Some departments that have been big contributors in the past hit some tough times, but my confidence in them is unshaken. I am convinced that we are going to have a quarter when every department is plus and then we will really give the shareholders a very pleasant surprise. Our potential earning power is awesome!

Itzhak Nanook Pumpernickanaylian pointed out to me that we all receive information or correspondence in Bear Stearns envelopes with a window. Nookie informed me that it is not against the law to re-use those envelopes. Just put the new salutation to the left of the window and be sure that the window is filled by the blank side of the material being sent. When it comes to saving money, those Eskimo-Iranian crossbreeds are something special.

We must continue to cut expenses. Please help me keep my job!

To	Senior Managing Directors Managing Directors Associate Directors	Date	February 20, 1990
From	Alan C. Greenberg	CC	

Subject Frequent Flyer Benefits

As you know, if you've ever tried to reach anyone around here, many of the people at Bear Stearns do an enormous amount of traveling.

I have been advised by Itzhak Nanook Pumpernickanaylian that all of this travel is producing a staggering amount of frequent flyer points. He suggested to me that perhaps the Firm could save an immense amount of money by using mileage points that Bear Stearns personnel earn on travel **for** Bear Stearns, **paid** for by Bear Stearns.

Therefore, I have instructed the Travel Department to reclaim all of the accrued mileage earned on firm-related business trips and use them towards all future Bear Stearns firm-related business trips.

From this day on, claim your frequent flyer mileage and turn the award certificates in to the Travel Department. They will use your free tickets (not upgrade certificates) for your future travels. This applies not only to all future travel, but also to all past travel.

The Travel Department will use all award certificates for free tickets. Employees are still responsible for monitoring their own accounts, as this will be done on an honor basis (with Uncle Ace observing the honorees).

This addition to our bottom line should have been picked up long ago, but even Nookie can drop the ball on occasion.

	Senior Managing Directors		
	Managing Directors		
To	Associate Directors	Date	March 14, 1990
From	Alan C. Greenberg	CC	

Subject

Do you have a problem with colleagues returning telephone calls? My definition of a problem is not returning your calls or a client's call **promptly**, or not at all.

If an associate has committed either of those insults, you have a choice. You can stew and complain to members of your immediate family, or you can call me **at once**. You will not be bothering me— on the contrary, you will make my day. Nothing makes me happier than helping (in a very gentle and kind way) a wayward employee relearn basic good manners.

I must admit that these educational meetings, usually held at teatime with crumpets, do test my self-control because I tend to dislike people who try to ruin the morale at Bear Stearns and try to indirectly bankrupt this golden goose.

	Senior Managing Directors Managing Directors		
To	Associate Directors	Date	March 23, 1990
From	Alan C. Greenberg	CC	

Subject

Today's newspaper devoted a lot of space to the fact that almost every Wall Street firm is drastically reducing its advertising budget. We are **not** reducing our budget one percentage point. In fact, our TV advertising may even increase from its present base, but in no case will it be lowered.

This action, by your Executive Committee, will not be a surprise to the associates who have been at Bear Stearns for several years. We have tried to be consistent in every action. Both Haimchinkel and Nookie think it is very important that the troops know what to expect. Being consistent may be dull, but it leads to a pleasant environment and to happy campers.

I enjoy working for a firm that is hiring—not firing—and in addition the firm is now committed to continuing its witty, elaborate and expensive ad campaign when other firms are retrenching. I hope you feel the same.

BEAR STEARNS

M E M O

To	Senior Managing Directors Managing Directors, Associate Directors Department Heads	Date	April 10, 1990
From	Alan C. Greenberg	CC	

Subject

We have built our business on certain principles and there are two axioms that must be repeated constantly to our associates.

We will not employ people who hide or bury trades, even if the delay is twenty-four hours. During the past year, we have had to terminate several people for this infraction. One person had worked as a trader at Bear Stearns for over ten years.

We will not employ people who ever disclose our or our clients' trading activity with **anybody** who is not authorized to have such information. Disclosing this to unauthorized people, who work either inside or outside Bear Stearns, will lead to immediate dismissal.

We have a very liberal policy of rewarding, with cash and promotions, personnel who help us improve this firm. If you want to become a lot richer, just give us information that will aid us in discovering employees who violate either of the two rules of behavior that I have just mentioned. Call your supervisor or me with any of your suspicions. You will never be criticized if your information proves to be inaccurate. The fable about the boy who cried "wolf" does not fit with the Bear Stearns philosophy. Cry "wolf" at every opportunity. If your doubts prove to be false, you will still be thanked.

Nookie asked me to comment about a particularly vicious rumor. It is **not** true that we are firing any of our jet pilots or company-employed chauffeurs. Any pilot or chauffeur who is **currently** employed by Bear Stearns has a job that is safer than mine. These rumors are getting so ridiculous that it would not surprise me if I heard that we are cutting our TV advertising budget.

MEMO

To	Senior Managing Directors Managing Directors Associate Directors	Date	May 9, 1990
From	Alan C. Greenberg	CC	

Subject

When summer arrives it seems that absenteeism increases. We need everyone on the job every day if we are going to keep our momentum going.

Nookie heard of my concern and he felt the matter of such importance that he consulted with his uncle, Haimchinkel Malintz Anaynikal. Their collective thoughts are listed below. Please note that I do not agree with all of their suggestions:

1. Sickness

    No EXCUSE . . . We will no longer accept your doctor's statement or note as proof. It is clear that if you are well enough to get to the doctor's office, you are well enough to come to work.

2. Leave of Absence (For an operation)

    We are no longer allowing this practice. We wish to discourage our associates from exposing any part of their body to a knife. Knives cut and cuts cause blood and that's bad.

    We hired you as you are and to have anything removed would clearly make you less than we bargained for. Therefore, anyone having an operation risks termination.

3. Death (Your own)

    This will continue to be a valid excuse, but we will now require a two-week notice since we will have to replace you.

BEAR STEARNS

M E M O

To: Senior Managing Directors
Managing Directors
Associate Directors

Date: June 8, 1990

From: Alan C. Greenberg

CC

Subject:

I have taken the liberty of reprinting a memo that was issued on July 17, 1989. It seems like some of our associates are reverting back to bad habits that could be corrected if they read the reprint.

"The in-house telephone operators are being swamped by our own associates dialing the Bear Stearns operator and asking to be connected to another Bear Stearns employee. All of us have been given Bear Stearns directories and we should dial the numbers ourselves. This will free up our operators to do constructive things like adequately servicing clients who are trying to reach our switchboard.

There are two reasons that the directories are not being used:

1. Laziness
2. Not being able to read

Nookie has suggested ways to handle both possibilities. The chief operator will keep a record of employees who need constant help from the operators. If those people are literate, they will meet with me.

For those associates who cannot read, we will have people on every floor with the designation of H.I.* If someone needs help in reading the directory, all they have to do is yell "HI" and help will arrive. This will not only improve our service, but could also increase the social life of the dumbbells.

This format should kill every cat in the alley."

* Code name for Helper of Illiterates.

M E M O

To	Senior Managing Directors Managing Directors Associate Directors	Date	July 10, 1990
From	Alan C. Greenberg	CC	

Subject

Another year has ended. Our results will be public knowledge in a few weeks and we can all be proud of last year for many reasons—including the fact that we are still here, stronger than ever.

I can guarantee very little about the future, but there is one thing you can bet on. Your executive committee is going to spend a lot of the new year stressing fundamentals. I do not think our success has been due to luck (although all of us welcome and appreciate good luck).

Football teams that are in great condition and can block and tackle, win. We are going to win because we constantly keep in mind certain axioms such as:

1). It is our job to inspire receptionists and secretaries to smile and sparkle when speaking to or seeing clients. The top people at Bear Stearns set an example by returning **all** calls promptly.

2). Avoid the herd mentality.

3). Control expenses—even more so in good times.

4). Every department should be staffed with the best and the brightest because I cannot tell you which area of our business will be "hot" six months from now.

5). Reduce expenses.

6). We are going to stick to the things we think we know something about. I am too old to start selling cars, costume jewelry or life insurance.

7). Conceit and complacency are dangerous, particularly in our line of work. If I ever feel that the people at Bear Stearns start thinking their body odor is perfume and I cannot convince them otherwise—I will sell my stock.

8). I like people who conduct their business "neat and clean." If you do not understand that, call me.

9). Cut expenses.

10). We must always be on guard in dealing with new relationships, and our associates must always be aware that we are watching the **shop** and them at all times. The best protection against in-house fraud is for management to have a great rapport with associates big and small. They will see aberrational behavior in a co-worker four years before internal audit spots the deception.

These guidelines are not exactly the Ten Commandments, but they did come via Haimchinkel Malintz Anaynikal (no relation to Moses) and we are going to live by them. I do not believe in fixing something that is not broken.

BEAR
STEARNS

M E M O

To: SR. MANAGING DIRECTORS,   Date: September 26, 1990
        MANAGING DIRECTORS
        AND ASSOCIATE DIRECTORS

From: ALAN C. GREENBERG

There is no question in my mind that people with no affiliation with Bear Stearns have been calling employees of Bear Stearns and misrepresenting themselves as co-workers. These impersonators have requested confidential information and have said "do not call me back, because I am very busy, but I will call you." They do call the low-level associates back and identify themselves as an important Bear Stearns Sr. Managing Director and try to get information that no one but a few Bear Stearns people should possess.

We are of course going after the firms these crumbs work for with every legal tool we can muster, but we must do more. All of us must impress on everybody we work with to beware of "do not call me, I will call you" inquiries. If they get one of those calls, and report it at once, they will simultaneously be showered with money (cash, loot, lucre, green stuff). Let people up and down the line see this memo.

We are in our own war with people who do not mind destroying our customer confidentiality to achieve their own personal goals. Haimchinkel Malintz Anaynikal pointed out to me that he has met some Russian roulette players that have won six or more bouts in a row, but he has never met a one-time loser at that sport. I do not like sports where if you are 11 for 11 and then lose one, you are out of business. That is where I feel we are now—we must win this one.

BEAR STEARNS

M E M O

TO: Senior Managing Directors   DATE: October 3, 1990
        Managing Directors &
        Associate Directors

FROM: Alan C. Greenberg

RE: <u>1990 Annual Report</u>

Our 1990 Annual Report is now out, and while the financial results have
been public for some time, they still make good reading. What really makes
the report noteworthy, however, is what we do not mention: no layoffs, no
discontinued businesses, no write-offs of bridge loans or double leveraging of
short-term borrowings. Instead we are able to stress the safety and strength
of our balance sheet and of our firm. In this era of uncertainty this puts us
in a unique position not only within the brokerage industry, but within the
entire financial community.

It may also interest you that since August 2, 1990 we have purchased
5,400,000 shares of Bear Stearns and retired them. Your Executive
Committee believes in Bear Stearns.

I encourage you to get a copy of the report, read it, and see that people in
your area see it. I further encourage you to share it with your customers
and make them aware that now, more than ever, they cannot afford not to
do business with Bear Stearns.

BEAR
STEARNS

M E M O

TO: Senior Managing Directors   DATE: October 17, 1990
       Managing Directors &
       Associate Directors

FROM: Alan C. Greenberg

You are correct. This is one tough period, and in my 41½ years in Wall Street I have seen a few. In fact, things are so bad, in almost every area, that Haimchinkel Malintz Anaynikal made an unexpected visit (he stressed that this was no reflection on the advice we have been getting from his nephew, Itzhak Nanook Pumpernickanaylian). Uncle Chinkel just felt that he might point out some factors that only experience can teach you.

1. The bear market will end and it can end quickly.

2. A bell will not ring to prepare you for the good times. Remember how great the world looked three months ago? The market can reverse its present course just as dramatically.

3. This market gives all of us a chance to demonstrate what we are made of. Some people go all through life and never get a chance to demonstrate their ability to lead. You are fortunate! You can help the people you work with to get through this by being a **leader**. Now is the time for real leaders to step up.

4. If you are going to stand tall, keep a few things in perspective. This is nothing next to Auschwitz, Buchenwald or Vietnam.

5. You are working for probably the most liquid firm in Wall Street and our firm, on a relative basis, looks stronger every day and we will keep it that way.

6. Haimchinkel Malintz Anaynikal pointed out that some people for ethnic reasons may get through this period easier than others. For example, I have never felt better or slept sounder, but I do have an advantage over some of my peers at other firms—I am the beneficiary of 5,000 years of persecution. This market will not get me down. It is just a minor challenge.

TO: Senior Managing Directors   DATE: December 6, 1990
           Managing Directors &
           Associate Directors

FROM: Alan C. Greenberg

It is official! The Strategic Planning Committee chaired by Bobby Steinberg and the Forward Planning Committee chaired by Barry Cohen have investigated the outlook for the Risk Arbitrage business and have come to a conclusion. We are going to **expand** our activity in risk arbitrage. The report by these two knowledgeable and unbiased gentlemen confirmed what your Executive Committee had felt all the time.

This inquiry into the economic feasibility of risk arbitrage was prompted by the fact that several major investment banking firms seem to be less than positive about the future of this activity. Your Executive Committee would have been negligent if it did not thoroughly and deeply study this ancient, arcane and mysterious art.

The complete report submitted to your Executive Committee is below:

"Au Contraire"

TO: Senior Managing Directors   DATE: January 10, 1991
         Managing Directors &
         Associate Directors

FROM: Alan C. Greenberg

Haimchinkel Malintz Anaynikal dropped by the other day and suggested to me that it was a good time to review some fundamentals. Pursuant to his wish, you will be receiving some subtle memos from me in the future, but I can assure you that my presentations will be more delicate than in the past because the direct approach did not seem to work.

Many years ago, your Executive Committee decided that all purchases of services were to be centralized to help us maximize our buying power. As an example: anything needed in the office had to go through Jim Lang's area. Any need for a lawyer had to be picked by Dave Glaser or Alan Schwartz. Anything needed for the repair and maintenance of the toilets had to be cleared with Alan Greenberg.

There is no such thing as an "approved" list. The fact that some plumber did a marvelous job for us in the past does not mean that an associate can take it upon himself to engage that person for new work. If you need a plumber, you must call me and I will decide who gets the next assignment.

I repeat, there is no "approved" list that people at Bear Stearns can initiate a call to. If you need the services of an accountant, lawyer, plumber, printer, etc., you must speak to the person that your Executive Committee has picked. You cannot make the choice.

If this memo is not clear, please call me directly and I will try to clear up your confusion.

TO: Senior Managing Directors   DATE: January 28, 1991
        Managing Directors &
        Associate Directors

FROM: Alan C. Greenberg

You have received several notices about the important meeting that is being held tomorrow afternoon in the auditorium at 4:15 p.m.

I think anybody with a drop of Jewish blood should show up. Your heritage will be taken into account if you make a pledge. For example, if you are only half Jewish, you only have to pay half of the pledge. If you are a quarter Jewish, you only have to pay a quarter of the pledge.

Israel is in a fight for its economic life, all they want from us is money.

M E M O

TO: Senior Managing Directors   DATE: January 31, 1991
        Managing Directors &
        Associate Directors

FROM: Alan C. Greenberg

If you were in the Bear Stearns auditorium on Tuesday afternoon, you participated in a thrilling and exhilarating experience.

In addition to getting people to pay their old pledges, U.J.A. Federation's Operation Exodus received $650,000 in new money from the Bear Stearns people.

The gifts ranged from $25.00 up to the thousands. Every gift was appreciated and I have never been prouder of my associates than I was yesterday. Thank you for setting an example that other firms can just dream about emulating. Bear Stearns has a reputation of giving to all causes that is well deserved.

Some of the gifts have come from people of very different religious and ethnic backgrounds. I wish to give those people a special thanks. It would be great if 100% of our fellow workers of a certain religious persuasion kicked in. The need is urgent and the cause is unique.

Let us set a record that can only be tied—100% participation by those with a touch or more of Jewish blood, from millicarons* to purebreds.

* Nookie's definition for those who are .0001% tainted: they can pledge $1,000,000 and according to the rules they only have to pay $1.00.

TO: Senior Managing Directors   DATE: February 8, 1991
        Managing Directors &
        Associate Directors

FROM: Alan C. Greenberg

Who said we are not flexible? It has been brought to the attention of your Executive Committee that some of our new hirees have trouble adjusting to one aspect of our culture. I am referring to our relentless quest to cut and watch expenses, exemplified by our refusal to buy paper clips and rubber bands.

We should have anticipated this culture shock because when a person joins us from a firm that has been losing billions, they should feel that we do things a little differently than the pack; but we do not want them to get the bends.

From this date forward, the Executive Committee is making the following concession: all new associates will receive a gift when they join Bear Stearns. This gift will be kind of a combination of a care package and a welcome wagon extravaganza. The personnel department has been told to give these new folks a paper bag with a box of paper clips and twenty rubber bands.

Please do not think for a minute that this represents a change in our basic philosophy. In fact, since business is booming we will once again emphasize cost control. Remember that great poker players leave **nothing** on the table when they hold good hands.

BEAR STEARNS

M E M O

TO: Senior Managing Directors and
Other Interested Parties

DATE: February 27, 1991

FROM: Alan C. Greenberg

An artist in Hawaii by the name of Ron Kent read about our charitable activities and donated a beautiful bowl to Bear Stearns. He asked that we have a lottery for this bowl, with the proceeds going directly to Operation Exodus.

The bowl is on display on the second floor of 245 Park Avenue on the aisle to the left of where I sit, and in front of the bell in the center of the trading floor. This circular bowl is handmade of wood and measures approximately 20" by 9". Because of the special Hawaiian wood it is made from, the color of the bowl contains many different shades of brown with a smooth finished texture.

If you would like to buy a lottery ticket, you can speak to Maureen or Lisa on extension 4608. The tickets will cost $25 apiece.

The bowl is worth $5,000 and we are going to limit the number of tickets sold to 10,000 (my perverted sense of humor could not pass up that opportunity). We will sell only 100 tickets.

BEAR STEARNS

M E M O

TO: Senior Managing Directors   DATE: March 28, 1991
Managing Directors &
Associate Directors

FROM: Alan C. Greenberg

Our third quarter ended on March 28th. Everybody who works here and is not comatose knows we are rolling!

The resolution of the Jardine dispute is a plus for a lot of reasons. The settlement was fair and a lot of people can now go back to working full time at their jobs at Bear Stearns.

Our dispute with Jardine is over with. I will never say a bad word about Jardine or its officers. If I hear of a Bear Stearns associate speaking ill of Jardine, I will be disappointed. In fact, my disappointment will only be tempered by a personal meeting with the loudmouth. We had a difference with Jardine and it is history. There is no upside in knocking anyone.

Whenever things go too well, I become very suspicious. This is one of those periods. Keep your guard up! Now is the time to be careful. Now is the time the dopes get knocked off.

Remember the rules and remember our culture. When business is good, we become careful with our capital and try to cut expenses.

1991–1995

We entered the decade of the '90s with a certain degree of apprehension. Although we had successfully emerged from three very difficult years in the strongest financial position in our history, no one could be sure what the new decade would bring. We believed we were well positioned to flourish if the markets continued their upward course, which they did. Bear Stearns' momentum surged beyond any of our expectations. We reported two consecutive record years in fiscal 1992 and 1993. Today our return on equity is the highest in the industry.

These memos reflect an important period in the history of the firm. Over the past three years, Bear Stearns has grown dramatically. Our employee count has surpassed 7,500 and our capital base stands at $7.1 billion. At the end of fiscal 1991 the firm employed 5,600 people and the capital base was $1.8 billion.

The senior management of Bear Stearns has been very careful to control the growth through a continued focus on certain fundamental principles. We are all very proud that those principles have enabled us to create one of the most profitable and entrepreneurial firms in the securities industry.

M E M O

TO: Senior Managing Directors   DATE: April 17, 1991
      Managing Directors &
      Associate Directors

FROM: Alan C. Greenberg

The earnings for the quarter ending March 31, 1991 are now history, but they do not come close to describing the past three months. I have been here 42 years and I cannot recall any period that comes close to the excitement and pleasure that those 90 days have given me. I hope that you have experienced the same feeling of exhilaration.

It is up to every one of us to keep our momentum going, but we must also keep all of our collective feet firmly on the ground.

During the Jardine trial, a memo of mine dated July 1987 was read into the record. The summer of 1987 was another time of euphoria for Bear Stearns (but nothing like this). The gist of the memo was that when things are too good something usually hits you right in the head.

The difference between us and the rest of the world is that we had the benefit of exposure to Haimchinkel Malintz Anaynikal in 1987 and now Itzhak Nanook Pumpernickanaylian. These two luminaries have done their best to remind us of the importance of never confusing body odor with perfume.

We must stick to the axioms that have guided Bear Stearns through some plenty tough years. If you know of some better rules, please let me know. If not, your Executive Committee is going to enforce the teachings with a vengeance. We like things that work—**THEY WORK.**

M E M O

TO: Senior Managing Directors   DATE: June 21, 1991
        Managing Directors &
        Associate Directors

FROM: Alan C. Greenberg

Our fiscal year is coming to a close and to say the least it was exciting. We started off slow, but the last six months showed our potential earning power.

Your executive committee has no surprises in store for the New Year. The prosperity in Wall St. has caused some of our competitors to start reaching for business, and once again we will decline to participate. Those of you who have been here for a while know that we will take tremendous risks if the fee justifies the exposure.

We have a reputation for watching expenses and that will not change. Nookie Pookie pointed out what happened to Egypt.* That will not happen at Bear Stearns.

On July 1, our New Year starts. The score is zero to zero. I would love to see us scorch the front nine. Historically the first six months of our fiscal year are difficult. Let us make this year different. I am an old man and I do not like pressure.

* 7,000 years ago the Egyptians were building pyramids and their women were riding in chariots, and getting manicures and pedicures (we know that from the paintings in the tombs). At that same time, the rest of the world was living in caves and chasing their next meal. The Egyptian civilization continued to advance for 5,000 years and then they started getting careless with expenses. Their overhead got out of control and that was that. They have been trying to recover for 2,000 years.

BEAR STEARNS

M E M O

To: Senior Managing Directors,   Date: August 13, 1991
         Managing Directors &
         Associate Directors

From: Alan C. Greenberg

We have been lucky!

During the roaring carefree period of Wall Street's latest excesses not one of Bear Stearns' senior managing directors has even received a subpoena much less been charged or accused of infractions relating to insider trading, stock parking, manipulation or other violations of this type. Yes, we have stressed the rules of conduct and behavior as codified by Haimchinkel Malintz Anaynikal. Yes, we have had the benefits of Nookie's on-spot inspections since Uncle Chaim retired, but we have also been lucky.

Some of our associates below the senior managing director level have strayed and they have paid dearly, but thus far top management has been squeaky clean.

We must make a concerted effort to keep it that way. I do not want to count on being lucky. All of us must talk to our co-workers about our respect for the rules. All of us must emphasize to our co-workers how they are being watched by us at all times (for their own good) and how severe our penalties are for infractions. I think it was Mark Twain who said, "fish stink from the head." The senior managing directors must set examples that leave no doubt about how we feel about morality and observance of rules—big or small.

I do not know of a firm of our size that comes close to our record of senior management compliance. We can all be proud, but we must not become complacent. We must not count on luck

BEAR
STEARNS

M E M O

TO: Senior Managing Directors,   DATE: August 14, 1991
     Managing Directors &
     Associate Directors

FROM: Alan C. Greenberg

Two important milestones were reached last week. McDonald's sold their 70th billion hamburger and Bear Stearns bought their 10,000th FAX machine.

I do have some sad news to report. The FAX machine salesperson who has serviced the Bear Stearns account has retired. He is burnt out—he is 33 years old. He has purchased Donald Trump's yacht, and the overworked soul just wants to cruise and take it easy for a while.

Nookie read this and thinks there is a moral hidden somewhere between the lines. Can you find it?

When we cut expenses we have a direct, equal and positive impact on our bottom line. If we forget this fact we will be a member of the "Losers Club" and stupid. That is one club that we are not joining.

BEAR
STEARNS

M E M O

TO: Senior Managing Directors,   DATE: August 26, 1991
        Managing Directors &
        Associate Directors

FROM: Alan C. Greenberg

We are having a problem getting a point across. Nobody below the level of Senior Managing Director is allowed to send any letters or signed material out of Bear Stearns unless the sender has shown the epistle to a Senior Managing Director and received his approval.

From this date forward any person who violates this simple rule will receive a very quick simple fine. Enough is enough—we have tried being Mr. Nice Guy—it did not work.

All of us receive various printouts and other printed matter every day from Bear Stearns. If you do not need the information or if the information should not be for you, call Pat Ripley 212-272-3271. Pat wil then do two things. She will stop the useless flow and also target you for a reward. If you do not cut off information you should not be exposed to, you will be fined.

Read this memo carefully, and be sure the people you work with understand our policy.

TO: SENIOR MANAGING DIRECTORS   DATE: NOVEMBER 11, 1991
       MANAGING DIRECTORS
       ASSOCIATE DIRECTORS

FROM: ALAN C. GREENBERG

Our business is great! Almost every department is contributing and maybe the prediction I made at the annual meeting is within sight.

There are three things I know for sure when we are in one of these cycles:

1) This period of euphoria will not last forever (neither I or any other human can accurately predict the end).

2) Humans tend to get sloppy when making money is easy.

3) Bear Stearns will <u>not</u> get caught up in the hysterical optimism and the people at Bear Stearns will <u>not</u> get careless or conceited.

It is the job of your executive committee to keep all of our feet on the floor. It is the job of your Executive Committee to see that we maximize the opportunities that we are being handed.

Remember, winning poker players squeeze every nickel out of good hands, and they do not tip cocktail waitresses $100—fools do!

Remember the simple axioms that have helped us in good times and bad. Having a great year is not going to change our culture!

– If we control expenses.
– If we diligently evaluate risks.
– If we hire carefully.
– If we run our business according to the highest level of morality.
– If we treat our associates the way we would like to be treated.
– If we return all telephone calls quickly and see that the people around us treat the clients with care.
– If we just use good common sense we can turn a great year into a <u>fabulous</u> one.

M E M O

TO: Senior Managing Directors   DATE: November 14, 1991
       Managing Directors
       Associate Directors

FROM: Alan C. Greenberg

The unsigned letter stapled to this memo was received by me a few days ago.

The page about "travel restrictions" seems a little tough, but I am by nature a softie. I will be making some random calls in the next few days to try to get a consensus about whether we should incorporate any of these suggestions into our culture.

November 7, 1991

Mr. Alan C. Greenberg
Chairman and Chief Executive Officer
Bear, Stearns & Co. Inc.
245 Park Avenue
New York, N.Y. 10167

Dear Mr. Greenberg:

While calling on your Whippany office last month, I came across a copy of your booklet, "Memos from the Chairman Volume II," which is great!

Having been forced to accept early retirement from an ailing investment banking firm last year, your prescriptions for cost-consciousness are most appropriate regardless of the economic climate. My former firm was guilty of most of the abuses Nookie is trying to eliminate.

I thought that you may want to pass along the enclosed memo to Nookie as it may give him food for thought in his ongoing quest to reduce expenses and contribute to Bear Stearns' viability.

Keep up the good work!

                    Sincerely,

                    An admirer of your management style who did not have
                    the good fortune to work at B.S. and is now selling
                    "small plastic roses."

Encl.

TO: ALL EMPLOYEES

RE: TRAVEL RESTRICTIONS

Due to budget constraints, the following corporate policies are announced regarding employees traveling on official business. These policies are effective immediately.

TRANSPORTATION

Hitchhiking in lieu of commercial transport is strictly encouraged. Luminescent safety vests will be issued to all employees prior to their departure on company business trips. Bus transportation will be used whenever possible. Airline tickets will be authorized for purchase only in extreme circumstances, and the lowest fares will be used. If, for example, a meeting is scheduled in Seattle, but a lower fare can be obtained by traveling to Detroit, then travel to Detroit will be substituted for travel to Seattle.

LODGING

All employees are encouraged to stay with relatives or friends while on company business. If weather permits, public areas such as parks and parking lots should be used for temporary lodging sites. Bridges may provide shelter in periods of inclement weather.

MEALS

Expenditures for meals will be limited to the absolute minimum. It should be noted that certain grocery chains, such as General Nutrition Centers and Piggly Wiggly stores, often provide free samples of promotional items. Entire meals can often be obtained in this manner. Travelers should also become familiar with indigenous roots, berries and other protein sources available at their destination. If restaurants must be utilized, travelers should seek establishments offering "all you can eat" salad bars. This will be especially cost-effective to employees traveling together, as a single plate can be used to feed the entire group. Employees are also encouraged to bring their own food while on company business. Cans of tuna fish, Spam and Beefaroni can be conveniently consumed at your leisure, without the necessary bother of heating or other costly preparation.

ENTERTAINMENT

Entertainment while on travel is strictly discouraged. If such extravagances are required on customer contacts, the customer should be encouraged to "pick up the tab." Such action will save the company money, and also convince the customer that we are concerned about spending money on providing a good product, not on useless frivolities. The hospitality provided to our customers who visit our facility shall also be tasteful, yet cost-effective. In lieu of extravagant dinners, a picnic bench will be placed in the parking lots near the dumpster and a garden hose will be made available so that liquid refreshments can be provided for our guests.

MISCELLANEOUS

All employees are encouraged to employ innovative techniques in our team effort to save corporate dollars. One enterprising individual has already suggested that money could be raised during airport layover periods which could be used to defray travel costs. In support of this idea, Red Caps will be issued to all employees prior to departure so that they may earn tips by helping other travelers with their luggage during such periods. Small plastic roses will also be made available to employees so that sales may be made as time permits.

BEAR STEARNS   **MEMORANDUM**

TO: All Traders   DATE: November 21, 1991

FROM: Alan C. Greenberg   CC:

= =

In the past I have written you about hiding trades or mismarking positions. Unfortunately, it's necessary to repeat the memo.

We were recently forced to fire a trader for mismarking positions in his trading account to conceal a loss. Let there be no misunderstanding: this is stealing and will not be tolerated. If you have a problem position, discuss it with the head of your desk. Absolution can be granted for losing money but never for lying about it.

All managers are responsible for making sure that this is understood by all of their traders and for delivering the message to all future employees.

BEAR STEARNS

M E M O

TO: Senior Managing Directors   DATE: December 5, 1991
       Managing Directors
       Associate Directors

FROM: Alan C. Greenberg

Nookie reminded me of something that should be automatic, but when we get busy people tend to get sloppy. Since a huge percent of our business is done over the telephone, telephone etiquette is very important.

When a phone rings, it should be answered promptly—if you keep clients waiting, they will and probably should call our competition. If you answer a call and it is not for you, be sure that your associate acknowledges your bringing the call to their attention by raising their hand—**eye contact means nothing.**

If you see a call on hold that seems to be blinking for a period of time, jump on and see if you can help the person or remind your co-worker that he or she has a call waiting.

There is nothing revolutionary about these suggestions; suggestions made by Haimchinkel Malintz Anaynikal and his nephew Nookie always seem simple, but so is gravity. Look how much publicity Hymie Newton milked out of that apple thing.

TO:	Senior Managing Directors	DATE:	January 15, 1992
	Managing Directors		
	Associate Directors		

FROM: Alan C. Greenberg

Bear Stearns just announced the most profitable quarter in its history. Industry conditions during the last three months were excellent, but my guess is we outperformed our peers.

Haimchinkel Malintz Anaynikal and Nookie over the years have encouraged us when things looked bleak and, conversely, they have warned us when things tend to get giddy. We are in a period now that will cause the stupid to get careless and overconfident, and the results are totally predictable—financial catastrophe.

The Executive Committee of Bear Stearns is committed to running the firm in the same dull, conservative, boring manner that seems to work. It is our hope that the people who work with us keep their feet on the ground and their heads level.

Almost every industry in this country is having financial problems. It is true we paid our dues by surviving and even prospering during some tough years for Wall Street, but do not confuse luck with brains. We must, as a firm and I hope individually, make the most of this euphoric period but give very little back when the curtain falls. I can promise you one thing—this picnic will not last.

BE CAREFUL, BE SMART, BE A SURVIVOR!

BEAR
STEARNS

M E M O

TO: Senior Managing Directors   DATE: January 21, 1992
       Managing Directors
       Associate Directors

FROM: Alan C. Greenberg

I just checked with Haimchinkel Malintz Anaynikal on a philosophical issue that has been bothering me. The question is two-pronged: "Should really rich people answer their own telephones and, if they are occupied when the call comes in, does an immediate return of the call by the millionaire show weakness or a dearth of committee meetings or a lack of attention to strategic planning?"

Haimchinkel Malintz Anaynikal had Nookie do some research. The results are conclusive and irrefutable. There is nothing in the Bible, Koran or Talmud that prohibits or encourages the slow answering of a distant yodel or the melodious squawk of a ram's horn (there were no telephones at the time those books were given or written). In addition, there are no governmental laws that Nookie could find (except for some new and old countries in Eastern Europe) that prohibit answering your own telephone or quickly returning a call. Just thought that these questions may have crossed your mind as they did mine.

There is one more item that bears thinking about. This is the time to really keep an eye on expenses. When you are involved in a month like the current one, it is easy to get sloppy. That is what makes us different—we watch expenses when business is great! If you turn out the lights when you leave your office, you will save a few pennies, but the example can save the firm big money. Fish stink from the head! The top people set the tone for the rank and file. Set an example that will make me giggle and gurgle.

BEAR STEARNS

M E M O

TO: Senior Managing Directors   DATE: March 17, 1992
        Managing Directors
        Associate Directors

FROM: Alan C. Greenberg

It is my sad duty to report the death of Christian K. Nelson at the age of 98. Christian Nelson, seventy-one years ago, dipped a slab of ice cream in chocolate and called it an eskimo pie.

This loss was taken particularly hard by Haimchinkel Malintz Anaynikal and his nephew, Nookie. Because as you know, their most revered holiday is Eskimo Pie Day.* It is, to them, the combination of Christmas and Yom Kippur.

Mr. Christian Nelson was not only an inventor; he was also many years ahead of his time in the area of human relations. Despite his name, he allowed people of all faiths to buy and eat his product. He was a true visionary and the holiday that he helped create will be observed forever by people of Irakimo heritage.**

* See memo dated October 4, 1988.

** The issue of an Iranian and Eskimo union.

BEAR STEARNS

M E M O

TO: Senior Managing Directors   DATE: March 30, 1992
      Managing Directors
      Associate Directors

FROM: Alan C. Greenberg

A few days ago, the New York associates of Bear Stearns at 245 Park were given the chance to have their eyes examined by the Glaucoma Foundation.

Here are the results. 563 people participated. Twenty-six had potential problems, two had serious problems and seven had glaucoma requiring immediate attention. These statistics are scary. We are going to see that every person in every office of Bear Stearns has a chance to get this examination. Glaucoma is a terrifying disease. Please see that the people in your area take advantage of this opportunity.

Good health is important to all of us and to the bottom line of Bear Stearns. Illness is expensive!

It is worth repeating that our policy on smoking is clear. No smoking anywhere at Bear Stearns except in your own office with the door closed. There will be no exceptions—unless you have worked at Bear Stearns more than **43 years.**

The front page of the Business section of Sunday's New York Times had an article about brokerage stocks. The article states, "the history of Wall Street is that surprisingly little filters through to the shareholders when times are good. The bosses raise their pay, perks seem to multiply, and lots of people are hired. It was supposed to be different this time, but if the new Salomon is acting this way, what about brokers not in the spotlight?"

Obviously, the writer is not familiar with Bear Stearns!

TO: Senior Managing Directors   DATE: April 23, 1992
         Managing Directors
         Associate Directors

FROM: Alan C. Greenberg

Bear Stearns is now being billed directly for electricity. Leaving lights or machines on when not necessary is burning money.

It will probably surprise you that I think burning money is stupid, and in addition, it is a direct hit to our bottom line. Some expenses are tough to cut but saving on electricity is easy, although it does require a little muscular coordination. Some non-athletes may have trouble making contact with a light switch while walking, but it can be done by almost anyone if you concentrate. In fact, after a little practice you will be able to throw a switch while walking fast. Make a game out of the ritual—see how many consecutive times you can flip the switch without missing.

Cutting expenses is the surest way to increase our earnings. If we all cooperate, maybe this concern for our profits will get our P/E multiple to seven.

Spread the word to the people in your area and then enforce the discipline.

TO: Senior Managing Directors   DATE: June 23, 1992
         Managing Directors
         Associate Directors

FROM: Alan C. Greenberg

Our year will be over in a few days. It was a record breaker and all of us should feel proud.

Bear Stearns has never been stronger or positioned as beautifully as we are at this moment. The teamwork that all of you demonstrated over the past twelve months was sensational and I think that factor was a big reason that we had such mammoth results.

I have been associated with Bear Stearns for many years and I can tell you that I have never been as optimistic about our future as I am at this time. Take a look at the people who have joined us recently. Take a look at the enthusiasm that radiates through every office. Take a look at the morale of the people around you—it is almost off the chart.

This place is rocking and our job is to keep it rolling. Everything is going our way. On July 1, 1992 the score is nothing to nothing. Join me in seeing that we set new records. If we have another record breaker, maybe we can get the multiple to six.

BEAR
STEARNS

M E M O

TO: Senior Managing Directors   DATE: August 13, 1992
         Managing Directors
         Associate Directors

FROM: Alan C. Greenberg

You are correct! It is exciting to be associated with Bear Stearns.

The first six weeks of our new fiscal year have been a continuation of last year's record-breaking performance. Top talent continues to join us and it looks like our head count will soon exceed the number we employed in October, 1987.

The only things that can stop our truly fabulous future are arrogance, ego and conceit. Bigger and more promising companies than Bear Stearns have been reduced to rubble by those easily acquired diseases.

The job of management is to spot these stupoveteers* and step all over them. We just cannot miss if we stick by the rules** and conduct** that got us to this party.

Our balance sheet has grown.

Our profits have grown.

Our employee numbers have grown.

We are going to be different—our hat sizes are going to remain the same.

* A clever new addition to the English language. The word is a combination of stupid, poverty and the three musketeers (arrogance, ego and conceit).

** If you do not know the works of Haimchinkel Malintz Anaynikal & Nookie, you are working for the wrong firm.

BEAR
STEARNS

M E M O

TO: Senior Managing Directors   DATE: October 9, 1992
    Managing Directors
    Associate Directors

FROM: Alan C. Greenberg

The first two weeks of October have come and gone. I may have had a more difficult 14 days, but frankly I cannot remember when.

An associate of many years has resigned, we settled a lawsuit for a ridiculous amount of money, the markets have been difficult and as a result we have had some trading losses that have not been fun.

I am not discouraged because luckily periods like this are covered by a saying of Haimchinkel Malintz Anaynikal, and I quote:

"You cannot fly with the eagles and poop like a canary."

Our losses have been taken, our minds are clearer and our job now is to get rolling in the right direction. The quarter is only fourteen days old!

BEAR
STEARNS

M E M O

TO: Senior Managing Directors   DATE: November 19, 1992
        Managing Directors
        Associate Directors

FROM: Alan C. Greenberg

These are tough times for many Americans and I am sure you receive as many resumes as I do.

I think we should all follow some simple rules. When we get a resume, either you or one of your associates should call the person who sent it to you and say that it was received and that it will be processed. If a resume is passed on to you for a final determination, it is essential that we notify the applicant that he or she has been accepted or rejected.

Will these procedures take a little time? The answer is yes. But if a member of your family was applying for a job wouldn't they appreciate these common courtesies? Remember one thing, today's applicant could be next year's client.

Using these simple considerations will make us stand out even more from the rest of the pack. Nobody ever said we were traditional and I am proud of it!

TO: Senior Managing Directors   DATE: February 5, 1993
        Managing Directors
        Associate Directors

FROM: Alan C. Greenberg

We need your help. Please help us get a message out to every associate. It is essential that <u>once again</u> we stress that we welcome every suspicion or feeling that our co-workers might have about something they see or hear that is going on at Bear Stearns that might not measure up to our standards of honesty and integrity. This should be a H.M.A.* crisis-control yellow warning.

We want people at Bear Stearns to cry wolf. If the doubt is justified, the reporter will be handsomely rewarded. If the suspicion proves unfounded, the person who brought it to our attention will be <u>thanked</u> for his or her vigilance and told to keep it up.

Forget the chain of **command!** That is not the way Bear Stearns was built. If you think somebody is doing something off the wall or his/her decision-making stinks, go around the person,** and that includes me.

Haimchinkel Malintz Anaynikal once said that a successful transaction has many fathers but a dumb decision is an orphan. We want our people to tell us of the boneheads or potential improprieties quickly! <u>Get these messages out loud and clear.</u>

---

* Abbreviation for Haimchinkel Malintz Anaynikal.

** We have had some senior people who resented "end runs." They quickly became associated with more conventional firms—you can draw your own conclusions about whether their career change worked out for the best.

BEAR STEARNS

M E M O

TO: Senior Managing Directors   DATE: February 12, 1993
     Managing Directors
     Associate Directors

FROM: Alan C. Greenberg

Haimchinkel Malintz Anaynikal just finished speaking at an important symposium held at Harvard for the CEOs of major U.S. corporations. His appearance created such a huge demand that Harvard had to restrict the attendance to officers from American companies that lost at least $3 billion last year. We did not meet the tough entrance requirements, but I did hear some things about his speech that I think bear repeating:

1. He is a strong believer that people who talk too much seem to have bad luck.

2. People who do not return phone calls promptly do not seem to make the grade at a highly profitable firm.

3. People who object to end runs will never make it in football, or with successful investment banking firms. Certain groups do need to observe a "chain of command" atmosphere, but highly motivated, intelligent people do not need this handcuff.

4. A firm that has enthusiastic receptionists and telephone operators starts off with a tremendous advantage over the dummies of the world. Keep in mind that the first impression people receive from Bear Stearns is with those associates.

5. If a business person has to ask his accounting department if he is making a profit, he will not be in business very long.

These five statements created an atmosphere of confusion and incoherence among the attendees. As a result, Harvard is being forced to invite the group back for workshops. These workshops will be led by Haim's nephew, Itzhak Nanook Pumpernickanaylian, and by Haim's twin nieces, the Meeskeit sisters —Salami and Pastrami.

Haimchinkel Malintz Anaynikal is not optimistic about his message getting through.

BEAR STEARNS

M E M O

To: Senior Managing Directors   Date: April 7, 1993
       Managing Directors
       Associate Directors
       All Department Heads

FROM: The Executive Committee

RE: **Dennis Hom**

Dennis Hom started to work at Bear Stearns in May 1987 at the age of 22. He progressed rapidly in Elliot Wolk's department and made many friends at Bear Stearns. Last week, Dennis was killed by an automobile as he was walking home from the train station. Dennis leaves a wife and two little girls.

The Hom family bought a home several months ago and there is a mortgage of $181,000 outstanding. The Executive Committee feels very strongly that this young family should not have to face the burden of this mortgage.

Many people have asked us what they could do for Dennis' family. Let us all participate in an old-fashioned mortgage-burning ceremony. Bear Stearns will pay $150,000 towards retiring this obligation and we think it should be easy to raise the balance from his associates at Bear Stearns. All checks should be made payable to the Dennis Hom Fund and sent to Elliot Wolk.

BEAR STEARNS

M E M O

TO: Senior Managing Directors   DATE: April 12, 1993
     Managing Directors
     Associate Directors

FROM: Alan C. Greenberg

Our earnings for the three months that ended March 31, 1993 were spectacular.

Fifteen years ago the Equity Capital of Bear Stearns was about 40 million (and we were rolling a big tax deferral). We earned $110,000,000.00 after taxes in the last quarter! That is amazing.

Our earning power has changed materially, but some things have not changed one bit:

1. We have no more layers of management now than we had in 1978.

2. We still realize the importance of trying to cut expenses.

3. We still realize how important it is to be on guard against conceit and arrogance.

4. We still are deeply concerned about the well-being of every person associated with Bear Stearns.

We have momentum and our morale has never been higher. Our future is unlimited as long as we remember where we came from and how we got this machine to its present level. Remember, Haimchinkel Malintz Anaynikal is watching. Step out of line or disregard his teachings and you will make that old man's day (and mine).

TO: Senior Managing Directors   DATE: April 15, 1993
         Managing Directors
         Associate Directors

FROM: Alan C. Greenberg

I had a call last week from Nookie congratulating the firm on our "best ever quarter." However, Nookie reminded me that "Pride goeth before a rap on the snout." He said that despite our revenues we still need to watch expenses like a hawk.

He told me, as an example, that those using laser printers and fax machines could get 5% to 10% more life out of the toner cartridges just by following the manufacturer's directions. When the toner is low, just take the cartridge out, shake it and give it another try. If we could get just 5% more use out of our toner cartridges, it would save the company $15,000 a year.

Nookie also mentioned that the folks who don't want to work for a living have come up with a new way to steal. Apparently, they call you and say they have a report of some kind of problem with your PC or Fax or some other kind of office equipment. They then ask for the serial number of the equipment. Shortly thereafter, they show up dressed in some kind of uniform and either want to take the equipment with them or work on it on-site. You know what happens next.

Should you experience something like this, call Security (x4333 at Park Avenue or x1147 at MetroTech) and alert them of the contact. They will take it from there. Needless to say, never let anyone work on your PC unless they can show you a valid Bear Stearns vendor ID.

Looks like Nookie is still at the top of his form. Please see that these thoughts get to every associate.

BEAR STEARNS

M E M O

To	All Employees	Date	May 12, 1993
From	Steve Lacoff	CC	

Subject

The attached letter was sent to Ace by Lisa Hom to be distributed to all employees. Please take a few minutes to read this beautiful thank you.

TO: All Employees

FROM: Lisa Ann Hom

I wish to extend my gratitude to the Executive Committee for the opportunity to address all of the employees of Bear Stearns.

As you may be aware, Dennis Hom, my husband, was a victim of a tragic automobile accident on the evening of March 24. He regrettably passed away on March 30 as a result of severe injuries from the accident.

Dennis, myself and our daughters, Jessica - 6 and Lauren - 4, had just moved from an apartment in Astoria, Queens into a new house we bought in Albertson, Long Island on March 6. I am sure if you have ever moved from one home to another, you are aware of the headaches and confusion you have with the logistics of moving. It seemed that all the problems that could have arisen happened to us.

Consequently, with such a short period gone by (approximately 2 weeks) from the time of our move up to the time of Dennis' accident, he didn't even have the chance to really consider obtaining mortgage life insurance for himself on the house. For the people who knew Dennis well, I'm sure you'll agree that this was something he would definitely have purchased very soon after our move. However, unfortunately for my family, he didn't have the opportunity to do so.

Therefore, I wish to offer a special thank you note to Alan Greenberg and the Executive Committee for their initiative and leadership effort on the drive to help us pay off the mortgage note on the new house. But equal thanks also goes to all of the employees of Bear Stearns.

And again, on behalf of my daughters and my entire family, we wish to express our deepest and most sincere "Thank you" and appreciation for the love, care and support you have shown to us during this most difficult and sorrowful period.

We cannot adequately express our heartfelt gratitude to each and every one of you, but please accept our most sincere feelings of appreciation and love. The concern and devotion provided to us by the employees of Bear Stearns is overwhelming and very comforting.

Your kindness and generosity will never be forgotten by this family. We are eternally grateful for the genuine care and concern you have expressed to us. I know my family's loving feelings and memories of Dennis will endure the test of time and will last forever in our hearts and minds. I hope you will also cherish your fondest memories of Dennis.

Finally, I am very grateful that Dennis had the opportunity to work with such wonderful, kind and caring people. We will always consider the people of Bear Stearns - not just as Dennis' fellow employees but very good and dear friends of our family.

BEAR STEARNS

M E M O

TO: Senior Managing Directors   DATE: July 1, 1993
           Managing Directors
           Associate Directors

FROM: Alan C. Greenberg

Another year has come and gone. It was probably the best twelve months in the history of Bear Stearns.

There are many things about 1993 that were gratifying, but the momentum we developed throughout the year and the way it seemed to reach a crescendo during the last quarter was thrilling. This place is jumping!

One of the basic laws of physics is that objects in motion tend to stay in motion. Your Executive Committee believes in physics, but it also believes in Haimchinkel Malintz Anaynikal. All of us have to work to keep this place rolling. Clients are not interested in our past triumphs (that is why 90% of our competition has disappeared over the past 20 years). Clients want service, ideas and tender loving care.

The new year is here and remember that records are made to be broken. Let us get ten runs in the first inning and then knock the cover off the ball!

TO: Senior Managing Directors   DATE: August 9, 1993
        Managing Directors
        Associate Directors

FROM: Alan C. Greenberg

About a month ago I congratulated all of you on the fiscal year that ended on June 30, 1993.

I pointed out that I would love to see us start fiscal 1994 with a bang and get a lot of runs in the first inning. July has come and gone; so it is possible to gauge your response to my request. Your efforts exceeded my wildest dreams!

In fact Itzhak Nanook Pumpernickanaylian (Nookie) expressed a fear that we might be peaking too early. Haimchinkel Malintz Anaynikal stepped in and explained that due to Nookie's inexperience he was confusing peaking with momentum.

Keep it up!

BEAR STEARNS

MEMO

TO: Senior Managing Directors   DATE: September 23, 1993
       Institutional Equity Department

FROM: Alan C. Greenberg

Dick Fay was a dear friend and colleague. Dick died a short time ago, and some of his friends and family are establishing the Richard J. Fay Scholarship Endowment Fund at Fordham University.

The goal is to raise $100,000 and they have so far received three pledges totaling $30,000.

If you would like to participate in perpetuating the name of a real friend, and at the same time helping qualified young people, please give Lisa D'Amore a call on x4608.

BEAR STEARNS

Dear Employee,

     In furtherance of its policy of encouraging charitable giving, Bear, Stearns & Co. Inc. is allowing the use of its office for the enclosed charitable solicitation. The Firm passes no judgement on the request or the organization involved. Participation is entirely voluntary. You should not feel any obligation or pressure to contribute. If you are not interested, simply ignore the request.

The Compensation Committee

BEAR STEARNS

M E M O

TO: Senior Managing Directors   DATE: September 24, 1993
        Managing Directors
        Associate Directors

FROM: Alan C. Greenberg

During the last few months the business community has been exposed to some new management tools. They are known by the cognoscenti as Total Quality Management (TQM), Continuous Improvement (CI), Business Process Reengineering (BPR) and Other Trading and Organizational Development Initiatives (OTAODI). Your Executive Committee is always looking for ways to improve our performance, and those titles intrigued us.

We appointed a committee (C) consisting of Haimchinkel Malintz Anaynikal (HMA) and Itzhak Nanook Pumpernickanaylian (INP) to do a comprehensive study. We thought you might be interested in the results. From now on we will use the jargon of advanced management.

The "C" discovered that we have lost 90% of our competitors over the last 20 years. Most of those managements were precocious; they were using those catchy techniques years ago.

> 35% used TQM
> 25% used CI
> 20% used BPR
> 10% used OTAODI

The remaining 10% did not use any sophisticated management tools, they were just extra special stupid.

The "C" suggested that we stick to common sense (CS) because catchy titles will never supplant "CS." If you disagree, you are working at the wrong place.

TO: Senior Managing Directors   DATE: September 30, 1993
          Managing Directors
          Associate Directors

FROM: Executive Committee

Investment Banking Firms have been plagued over the years by traders mismarking positions, and we have not been spared. My guess is that the miscreants are hiding a loss they hope will go away, but as you know, the loss usually gets bigger and the result is bad. It is a tribute to the overriding strength of our business that we have been able to absorb these crimes and still prosper, **but this negative vigorish must be stopped.**

For the past months the heads of every department on Mondays have warned the troops of the danger of mismarking. We are now adding an additional refinement to the process. Consistent with our goal of trying to help everybody at Bear Stearns to become richer, we will give five percent on the spot to any person in the trading areas who alerts us to a potential negative mismark. If the mismark shows a loss of one million dollars, the cooperating person will get $50,000 immediately.

All suspicions will be treated confidentially. If one wishes to call Mark Lehman (ext. 2549), instead of someone in his/her own area, that is fine. No one will ever be criticized for false alarms.

We would frown upon the tattler sharing the reward with the mismarker based on some prearranged plot.

TO: Senior Managing Directors,   DATE: October 25, 1993
         Managing Directors
         and Associate Directors

FROM: Alan C. Greenberg

On June 12, 1983, the <u>New York Times</u> had a rather large article about Bear Stearns. There were a couple of quotes in the piece from our competitors that we took umbrage with and told them in writing what we thought. Below is one of the quotes.

> " 'Bear Stearns has done an intelligent job of seeking segments that most people found to be too small, specialized or even vaguely repellent,' said George L. Ball, president and chief executive officer of <u>Prudential-Bache Securities</u>. 'Most firms will, at times, forgo profits for reasons of perception. But Bear Stearns has the idea that a legitimate transaction is one that earns a dollar—even if it's something you don't want to bring home for dinner with mother.' "

As Haimchinkel Malintz Anaynikal has mentioned so often, "what comes around goes around." Nookie added something that was particularly poignant—"you meet the same people on the way down that you met on the way up."

We have constantly stressed that people at Bear Stearns do not denigrate our competition. Your Executive Committee wants to reemphasize that position. <u>If you cannot say something nice about somebody, do not say it!</u>

TO: Senior Managing Directors,   DATE   December 15, 1993
      Managing Directors &
      Associate Directors

FROM: Alan C. Greenberg

According to the press, it is getting harder and harder to run a large business. Your Executive Committee was making every effort to understand the new management tools. I am speaking of:

1. Reengineering
2. Total Quality Management
3. Economic Value Added

It now appears that, and I quote from a prominent business weekly, "Hierarchy is dying. In the new corporate model, you manage across—not up and down."

This statement seems to me to have many ramifications, including several new models for the corporate chart. Because things are changing so quickly in corporate management, we have decided to delay our study of the new techniques, stand back and wait for things to sort themselves out. Maybe the business school gurus will come to the conclusion that the best business management tool is common sense and look at all the time we will have saved.

I have always thought that because of our management style we have a chance in life, and after reading the current nonsense I am convinced that we will continue to be even bigger winners, if we continue to:

1. Watch expenses
2. Work for our clients
3. Keep our feet on the ground and our heads on straight.

Our results will continue to amaze the business schools and maybe they will try to figure out our revolutionary methods (they will not be able to).

TO: Senior Managing Directors,   DATE: March 11, 1994
           Managing Directors &
           Associate Directors

FROM: Alan C. Greenberg

If you answer a telephone at Bear Stearns, you are very important to our present and to our future. Your voice and enthusiasm represent the first impression many people get of Bear Stearns. This is not the first memo I have written about the importance of these people, but I get the feeling that a certain slippage has developed.

Last week Nookie unfortunately got involved with somebody with the personality of a wet noodle who used the expression "that is not my area" and dropped him. We are looking for enthusiastic, helpful, short-hold times, quick transfers, in other words, people who try.

Attached is a brochure that made me once again think of the subject. It was not written by Haimchinkel Malintz Anaynikal, but it could have been. Please see that everybody in your area reads* this pamphlet.

WE ARE GOING TO PROJECT A POSITIVE TELEPHONE IMAGE!

* If some of your highly paid key people cannot read, please read it to them—it is a very short document.

TO: Senior Managing Directors,   DATE: April 19, 1994
          Managing Directors &
          Associate Directors

FROM: Alan C. Greenberg

It is working! Attached is a memo which is dated September 30, 1993. Please reread it and you will get my point. There has been one refinement. In no case will the reward exceed $1,000,000. This will discourage slow reporting based on the free option principle.

During the last two months, we have distributed two checks to people who reported mismarkings; the last one was for $65,000.00. In both cases the recipients were reporting certain lapses of their bosses, so not only did they get a check, but they received an immediate promotion because their bosses no longer work for us.

This was a collateral feature that I did not think of in my original memo, but I think every associate of ours should now realize they have an added incentive for watching the conduct of the people they work for.

In my particular case, I have noticed a recent amount of tremendous curiosity, attentiveness and attention lavished on me by Lisa and Maureen.

M E M O

TO: Senior Managing Directors,   DATE: May 9, 1994
        Managing Directors &
        Associate Directors

FROM: Alan C. Greenberg

The markets are rather turbulent and we do a lot of business in securities that are not listed on national exchanges, such as over-the-counter securities, some bonds, mortgages and derivatives. It is very important that clients who own these securities and call us for an indication of the market be given the most accurate prices that we can determine.

Some recent publicity has suggested that salespeople at another firm were afraid to reveal to a client the drop in value of a security. If we ever feel that one of our salespeople, because of pressure from the client or his or her own stupidity, gives a client a market indication that masks the true picture, we will take the following action. We will ask the salesperson personally to buy $1,000,000 worth of securities at the overly optimistic price.* There will be no fines, just this simple transaction followed by a disciplinary meeting with very senior people.

If I were a salesperson, I would be very sure that the indication that I gave to the client came from an authorized person on the trading desk. If that procedure is followed and the price indication is wrong, the salesperson is absolved.

* If the market at the time of discovery is higher than when the fictitious quote was given, the salesperson will just have the pleasure of the meeting.

BEAR STEARNS

M E M O

TO: Senior Managing Directors,   DATE: May 24, 1994
       Managing Directors &
       Associate Directors

FROM: Alan C. Greenberg

Two Bear Stearns employees have called me within the last 24 hours complaining about the failure of other Bear Stearns people to return phone calls promptly. The shy, little complainers would not give me the names of the miscreants, which of course denied me the joy of speaking to the culprits.

There are a lot of things about our business that are difficult and some things are out of our control, but returning phone calls is something we can control. We have had a lot of new people join our organization during the past year and maybe they are not aware of how strongly we feel about returning phone calls from clients and associates. During the business day every phone call should be returned promptly, even if the person is selling malaria. What people do about returning phone calls that come to their home is something out of our control (I return all phone calls as soon as I can regardless of where I am domiciled).

I can only repeat what I have said before. If you want to really make my day and give me pleasure which I am probably not entitled to, just let me know when somebody at Bear Stearns does not return a phone call promptly. You will also be helping us stay ahead of our competition. They are too involved in long-term strategic planning to worry about something as silly as returning calls.

TO: Senior Managing Directors,   DATE: July 20, 1994
          Managing Directors &
          Associate Directors

FROM: Alan C. Greenberg

Today's <u>New York Times</u> disclosed that a major company has declared "matrix management in our company is dead." The president of that company said "that statement is monumental." I must admit that the company involved with that style of management cannot be faulted for not giving it a fair trial because over the last four years this tool has helped them lose four billion two hundred million dollars.

The company is now going to try putting in place "a system that makes its top executives more clearly accountable for the success or failure of their divisions. No more interminable meetings before making decisions. No more delays in replying to a customer's call for help." This article made me realize how stupid I am because I did not know there was any other way to run a business but to make people accountable, make timely decisions and service the client.

Another year has come and gone. It was exciting and certainly one of our better efforts. We had major disappointments from certain associates, but maybe it will help us run a tighter shop. Our goal still remains—a high return on equity with integrity.

I hope you are looking forward to the new year with as much enthusiasm as I am.

TO: Senior Managing Directors,   DATE: July 28, 1994
        Managing Directors &
        Associate Directors

FROM: Alan C. Greenberg

The Bear Stearns figures for the year ending June 30th are now history. The fact that our earnings for the year set a new record was rather hidden by the press because our fourth quarter was down versus last year. All of us would have preferred that our fourth quarter would have been the first quarter so we could have showed a nice progression, but we have to play the cards that we were dealt and it certainly was a tremendous year.

A few years ago index arbitrage was accused of everything from the bear market to tornadoes. It was a conclusion based on ignorance and we took a definite stand for what we thought was a very legitimate part of the business. When was the last time you heard a criticism of index arbitrage? We are hearing the same negative things now about derivatives.

There is a risk in everything you do and that certainly includes derivatives and personal relationships. I think one should always be careful in whatever the person is involved with. My personal point of view is that people should certainly stay involved in both—derivatives and personal relationships.

BEAR STEARNS

M E M O

TO: Senior Managing Directors,   DATE: August 17, 1994
      Managing Directors &
      Associate Directors

FROM: Alan C. Greenberg

Over the years we have tried to stress that the best security system is alert associates. Internal Audit will probably catch the miscreants in the long run, but that could take years. A perfect example of what we hope for happened last week.

Margaret Kelly and Evelyn Hall are administrative assistants working in the Futures Department. One of their responsibilities is to monitor the department's usage of taxicab vouchers. In checking last month's invoices, they discovered several vouchers signed by persons not employed in their area. After checking the names with Personnel, it was determined that the names on the vouchers were totally fictitious!

Margaret and Evelyn took the initiative to contact the taxi company to determine from which telephone extensions the questionable car transportation was ordered. Using this information, they were able to identify a suspected employee. They then arranged for a taxi driver associated with a questionable voucher to come up to the office and positively identify the suspect as his passenger. Once this was accomplished all details were provided to Security, resulting in the termination of the employee. Margaret and Evelyn received a cash award on the spot.

Please see that the people in your areas hear about this. You can also reiterate our reward policy regarding reporting a colleague's mismarking of a position. There are all kinds of ways to make money at Bear Stearns.

TO: Senior Managing Directors,   DATE: September 29, 1994
        Managing Directors &
        Associate Directors

FROM: Alan C. Greenberg

There was an article in the <u>New York Times</u> this morning about a man living in Atlanta who ripped off every brokerage firm that had an office in that area to the tune of about $15 million. Bear Stearns is conspicuous by its <u>absence</u>. We were not among those who got hit by Mr. Morse.

It is not a case of being lucky; it is a case of Mike Margolis, Frank Cox (the broker) and Floyd Berger (compliance) declining to do business with Mr. Morse after his first trade with us. Even though Mr. Morse fulfilled his obligations on that transaction, the boys declined to participate in any further dealings with Mr. Morse—something did not pass the smell test. Our people demonstrated the type of suspicion, skepticism and cynicism we want to see in the people at Bear Stearns.

When acting as a broker we are working for a very small commission so our upside is limited. In all cases there is huge risk if our judgment is wrong. **Nice going guys!**

TO: Senior Managing Directors,   DATE: October 13, 1994
          Managing Directors &
          Associate Directors

FROM: Alan C. Greenberg

The following is an excerpt of an article that appeared in the <u>American Banker</u> on October 6, 1994.

> "The government is denying a report that it is investigating some of the biggest brokerage firms in the country for money-laundering violations.
>
> The Wall Street Journal reported on September 21 that Merrill Lynch & Co., Dean Witter Discover, Inc., Prudential Securities Inc., Paine Webber Group Inc., and Bear, Stearns & Co. are being investigated by the U.S. Customs Service and the Internal Revenue Service for illegal activity involving wire transfers.
>
> 'There is no investigation' of these companies, said Marvin Smilon, spokesman for the U.S. Attorney's Office for the Southern District of New York. While Mr. Smilon said he usually would tell a reporter 'no comment' in such a case, he said he was afraid it would be construed as an affirmation of the story."

I am sure when you read the <u>Wall Street Journal</u> article on September 21st, you were as upset as I was. We were never called to comment on the allegations prior to the publication. The facts are that Bear Stearns does not take in sizable amounts of cash for any account. The government did examine some accounts <u>several</u> months ago that had money wired into them via commercial banks. We had never heard another word until the article was published on September 21st.

It is a shame that the article in <u>American Banker</u> did not get the same coverage that the negative article did, but I guess that is life in the big city.

BEAR STEARNS

M E M O

TO: Senior Managing Directors,   DATE: October 25, 1994
Managing Directors &
Associate Directors

FROM: Alan C. Greenberg

It is important that the management of Bear Stearns keep up-to-date on the latest buzz words. If you look at my memo dated September 24, 1993, it discussed:

- Total Quality Management (TQM)
- Continuous Improvement (CI)
- Business Process Reengineering (BPR)
- Other Trading and Organizational Development Initiatives (OTAODI)

I just received a pamphlet describing Value Migration and how to profit from it. At first glance I thought the article referred to bird watching, but since I know of no bird named value, my curiosity was aroused.

I am not going into how stupid the thoughts are, but I did want you to know about this latest management technique so if the phrase is ever brought up in your presence, you can nod and say that you certainly heard of this latest innovation. You can refer to it in the future by using its code name:

- Value Migration (DUM)

146

BEAR STEARNS

M E M O

TO: Senior Managing Directors,   DATE: October 28, 1994
         Managing Directors &
         Associate Directors

FROM: Alan C. Greenberg

The timing of the memo with regard to Value Migration dated 10/25/94 was perfect!

I have just received an invitation from Corporate Decisions Inc. of Boston to attend a one-day Senior Executive Forum on November 29, 1994. The subject of the conference is: **Value Migration: A Strategic Framework for Succeeding in the 1990s.**

If any of our senior managing directors would like to participate, please let me know. They will not be allowed to attend, but I would like to discuss with the interested parties why they want to attend, their philosophy of managing and why they are at Bear Stearns. My direct number is x4605.

It seems like we receive at least one invitation a week to attend a conference regarding the buzz words described in the 10/25/94 memo. I find it amazing that we never hear of a conference devoted to applying <u>common sense</u> to the securities industry. <u>We cannot miss.</u>

BEAR
STEARNS

M E M O

TO: Senior Managing Directors,   DATE: January 23, 1995
        Managing Directors &
        Associate Directors

FROM: Alan C. Greenberg

The current <u>Businessweek</u>, dated January 30th, has an article about a book published two years ago that has sold two million copies in 14 languages. The title is <u>Reengineering the Corporation</u>. If you followed my advice, you did not read the book and you saved yourself time and money because the author is now putting out a new book stating that reengineering is in trouble!

The writer concludes that the main reason reengineering is not working is because of the shortcomings of management. The author goes on to say that unless managers know how to "organize, inspire, deplore, enable, measure and reward value-adding operational work, reengineering will not work." What a surprise. Haimchinkel Malintz Anaynikal learned that in Goat Herding 101 (kindergarten in his country).

These are tough times and there is no easy fix. We have followed certain rules and policies over the years and we know they work. They will work in this environment, and we will come through stronger than ever.

BEAR STEARNS

M E M O

TO: Senior Managing Directors,   DATE: January 27, 1995
Managing Directors &
Associate Directors

FROM: Alan C. Greenberg

A number of sales people, in all areas, have asked us to hire a market technician. I have discovered somebody that I think will satisfy everybody including those in charge of our long-standing austerity program. This man will work literally for peanuts.

All we have to supply him with is paper and pencil and Doodles Danenberg will do his job. We will then distribute his graphs, which I promise you will be as good as any technical work done on Wall Street.

Doodles will not be housed at 245 Park Avenue, but will be available for personal consultation if you wish. His residence is a few blocks away. He is a chimpanzee residing at the Central Park Zoo.

I am sure all of you wish Doodles the best of luck. He will report to Mark Kurland.*

* Mark mentioned to me that thus far Doodles has been less demanding than any addition he has made in the last five years. There is a moral here. All of us should think of broadening our new-hire horizons.

BEAR STEARNS

M E M O

TO: Senior Managing Directors,   DATE: May 24, 1995
     Managing Directors &
     Associate Directors

FROM: Alan C. Greenberg

We are very fortunate, all of us are working in a fascinating, dynamic organization. We have hired some exciting new people throughout the firm and they have become acclimatized in record time.

Some departments that the press had written off are coming on like gangbusters and we are close to running on all cylinders. Our business is great!

I do have a wish—my hope is that our overall business grows at the same percentage as our error account, which is accelerating at a record rate. The errors are very democratic; they are committed by people up and down the line. If you did an autopsy, you will find that in almost every case people are just plain careless. Putting in buys instead of sells or entering 5 option contracts instead of 50. We have got to do something about this expense because it comes right off our bottom line. If you have any suggestions, please let me know. You must make a point of discussing this problem with the people in your area.

I expect to see a major improvement (the last time I broached this subject the errors went up, but I thought I would try again) within hours of this epistle reaching our co-workers.

BEAR STEARNS

M E M O

TO: Senior Managing Directors,   DATE: June 12, 1995
           Managing Directors &
           Associate Directors

FROM: Alan C. Greenberg

A great number of our associates have dropped me notes telling me of excess reports and statistical material that they have received and that they feel are unnecessary. In some cases, people at 245 Park Avenue have received documents from Bear Stearns through the regular U.S. mail. I am sure that a lot of money can be saved if we stop this wastefulness.

We are going to try to centralize and investigate every incident of surplus paper that is reported to us. The person to call is Steve Wexman on x2-6060.

Thanks for your past consideration and let us see if Steve can bring order out of this chaos.

TO: All Employees   DATE: July 31, 1995

FROM: Alan C. Greenberg

I believe there is a direct correlation between telephone etiquette and earnings. We recently hired a consulting firm to investigate how quickly we answer our telephones and how we treat callers who dial our numbers by mistake.

The good news is that most employees are accessible and answer their own telephone within two rings. The bad news is that some of our calls go unanswered, that many employees' telephone greetings either sound rude or are unintelligible and **that 26% of all employees are unable to properly transfer a call.**

We have never hired people based on muscular coordination, but maybe we should change our policy since transferring a call seems to require more athletic ability than some of our associates possess. Be prepared for spot checks on your telephone transferring capabilities; you will be judged 10% on speed and 90% on accuracy. Those who flunk will get private lessons from me.

It appears that in all of the recent excitement, some of you have forgotten that the way you answer your telephone may be the first—and last— impression the caller gets of Bear Stearns. Please don't forget again. From this day forward, I expect you to know how to transfer a call and also to be pleasant when answering your telephone every time it rings.

TO: Senior Managing Directors,   DATE: August 25, 1995
          Managing Directors &
          Associate Directors

FROM: Alan C. Greenberg

During the summer, Fridays are usually quiet—lonely in the office—but quiet. Today was an exception.

An associate of ours who retired in 1990 had asked our personnel department for some information and she wrote me a letter and told me that they did not answer her <u>many</u> inquiries. A former registered rep in San Francisco said that the compliance department of Bear Stearns in San Francisco did not return his calls. A registered rep in Los Angeles called me and told me a client of his had called the mortgage operations in Dallas and a young lady there did not return his <u>calls</u>. It is hard to believe that with all the emphasis we have put on the importance of returning phone calls these three incidents should surface on one day.

There are usually three sides to every story, but it was hard for me to find the side that puts our people in the right. I spoke with the areas in Bear Stearns that seem to be less than perfect and I hope I ruined their weekend because I tried very hard to.

Do you realize what a negative effect not returning a call has on an associate or a client?

Using the English language as a prod has not worked. From now on, fines will be levied on lazy, inconsiderate non-phone call returnees. Please inform the people who work with you of the new policy.

If you or your clients suffer any "telephone indignities," please call me. It will make my day.

TO: Senior Managing Directors,   DATE: September 1, 1995
        Managing Directors &
        Associate Directors

FROM: The Executive Committee

Prior to the end of our fiscal year, we had 256 Senior Managing Directors. We always have some attrition at this time of year and losing eight managing directors (3%) would not have caused much discussion, but six who retired worked in approximately the same area. Because of this, there has been a lot of comment and publicity about these changes, and there will probably be more.

The Executive Committee would like to point out that the mortgage area is certainly not what it was in terms of profitability. The profits of the department, and therefore the bonuses in that area, are down considerably versus several years ago.

None of the six individuals who left did so to go to a competitor. In fact, none of them had immediate plans to go anywhere.

Most of the people who left felt that the future of that area was rather limited—our opinion is the opposite. A few years ago people in general had written off the prospects of high-yield bonds and they were wrong. A few years ago that world had written off bank stocks and we do not have to tell you what these "interest-sensitive companies" have done. Remember that cliche? While others have reduced their commitment to the mortgage business, we remain dedicated to it, and our competitive position has never been stronger. <u>The big profits in the mortgage area will be back.</u>

We suggest that you use these thoughts if people question you about recent events.

TO: Senior Managing Directors,   DATE: September 27, 1995
     Managing Directors &
     Associate Directors

FROM: Alan C. Greenberg

A prominent consulting group just sent me an invitation to attend their fifth North American Financial Services Conference. One of the topics that they are using to entice attendance is "*Reintermediation May Pose As Big A Challenge In The Nineties As Was Disintermediation In The Eighties.*" I think I am going to resist participating in that get-together because I do not have any idea what they are talking about.

I could not wait to get to the office this morning and talk to the head of our Internal Audit department. I want all bank balances and security positions that are held away from Bear Stearns to be spot-checked on a surprise basis many times a quarter. If we do this, it is hard for me to see how a billion dollars can disappear.

When a consulting group sponsors a symposium that discusses mundane subjects like how to stop money from flying out the front door or how to get associates to cut expenses and return telephone calls, then I will be one of the first to sign up.

BEAR
STEARNS

M E M O

TO: Senior Managing Directors,   DATE: November 13, 1995
         Managing Directors &
         Associate Directors

FROM: Alan C. Greenberg

The media has been having a field day with the problems of Daiwa Bank. Quoting from *NEWSWEEK*, "It wasn't that the Daiwa dummies lost $1.1 billion; it is that they lied about it and dissed the Fed. It doesn't pay to get too arrogant."

This was not the first time nor will it be the last that we have seen what arrogance can lead to. This danger has been pointed out many times to all of us by Haimchinkel Malintz Anaynikal; it should be brought to the attention of our associates on a regular basis. Our job is to look out for arrogance and stomp on it every time we see its ugly head rearing up.